Refugee Countess

The Five Lives of

Marion Stein

Refugee Countess

The Five Lives of

Marion Stein

JANET TENNANT

T

The manufacturer's authorised representative in the EU for product safety is Authorised Rep Compliance
Ltd, 71 Lower Baggot Street, Dublin D02 P593 Ireland
(www.arccompliance.com)

Troubador Publishing Ltd
Unit E2 Airfield Business Park
Harrison Road, Market Harborough
Leicestershire LE16 7UL
Tel: 0116 279 2299
Email: books@troubador.co.uk
Web: www.troubador.co.uk

ISBN 978 1 83628 179 5

British Library Cataloguing in Publication Data.
A catalogue record for this book is available from the British Library.

Printed and bound by CPI Group (UK) Ltd, Croydon, CR0 4YY
Typeset in 12pt Minion Pro by Troubador Publishing Ltd, Leicester, UK

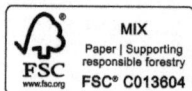

MIX
Paper | Supporting
responsible forestry
FSC
www.fsc.org   FSC® C013604

To my partner Keith,
Kirsty, Anna, Luke and Olivia
With love

Contents

Preface

I first came across Marion Stein when reading early volumes of letters by the composer Benjamin Britten. My partner was writing a book on 20th century British composers and Britten was of key interest. I was aware from the warmth in the letters to Marion or her father that this woman, a friend of his from her childhood, meant a great deal to him. In her teenage years Marion and her parents had lived in London with Britten and his partner Peter Pears.

From those early years until he died, she wrote to him, almost as to an older brother, for advice and his comfort at difficult times in her life. He valued her opinion as both a musician and a friend.

Then, just a short time after reading Britten's letters, I read the book, *A Very English Scandal* and saw the television series of the same name. Here I met Marion again. I was intrigued by this woman who, in 1973, married Jeremy Thorpe the Liberal Party Leader despite rumours of his homosexuality.

I realised that these two Marions, in whom I had become so interested, were the same person. I was eager to find out how the young friend of Benjamin Britten became Mrs Jeremy Thorpe.

I found that Marion's life between being Marion Stein and Marion Thorpe involved her escape from Nazism in Vienna, becoming a musical prodigy, forming close and lasting friendships with the musical elite, becoming a Royal Countess, and enduring marital and criminal scandals. Throughout all this, she contributed so much to the musical life of the country as to be awarded the CBE for services to music in 2008.

I wanted to tell her story.

Introduction

Sometime in the 1990s.

A smart, straight-backed older woman pushes a man in a wheelchair through Kensington Gardens. Those familiar with the couple's daily routine might smile at them or exchange a greeting. Casual passers-by glance towards them idly, in the same way as they would any other feature of the park, a tree, a passing cloud. And then they look again. They recognise in this man, something in his face, his jaunty hat. Something they know from way back. From newspapers? from television?

Perhaps when the chair and its occupant have long since passed, they realise that the man in the chair is Jeremy Thorpe, many years ago the leader of the Liberal Party. They may remember his sparkling potential, his ebullience, his colourful personality. But they may also remember the allegations of his homosexuality at a time when such acts were illegal, the scandal of his trial for conspiracy to murder, his widely unexpected acquittal and his subsequent fall from grace.

They are unlikely to pay much attention to his companion, lovingly attentive. His wife, Marion Thorpe.

Perhaps they should. This is a woman whose life was even more varied than that of her husband.

Her life was one of contrasts.

From a refugee from Hitler to a career as a concert pianist, from a suburban life in London to that of a countess with an 18C mansion in Yorkshire and large London home. From the intimate friend of Benjamin Britten to knowing many of the world's great musical artists. From the mother of grown sons in swinging London, to the stepmother of a small boy. From short and newly found happiness as a political wife to being engulfed in a nationwide scandal. From a support and help for her disgraced and increasingly invalid husband, to recognition for her services to music by the CBE.

Somehow, Marion has stayed 'under the radar.' When mentioned in books about the great and the good (and the questionable) she is usually defined in relation to men. She is a daughter, a mother, a friend, a wife, a colleague. The real woman kept her counsel. At least usually in public. However, her influence on people and events is there to be seen if one cares to look.

List of Illustrations

Unless otherwise attributed, all illustrations are by kind permission of the Earl of Harewood.

1. The apartment of the Stein family in Vienna

2. Erwin Stein as a young man

3. Erwin Stein with friends, composers Anton Webern and Arnold Schoenberg, 1920s

4. Marion Stein aged about 11, Vienna

5. Marion Stein, concert pianist, by David Gurney, Associated Press. © National Portrait Gallery, London

6. Marion Stein on the day of her engagement to George Lascelles. 19 July 1949

7. Marion Stein with George Lascelles 19 July 1949

8. Wedding of Marion Stein to George Lascelles, 7th Earl of Harewood, 10 November 1949

9. Harewood House, West Yorkshire (Author)

10. The family home at 2 Orme Square, Bayswater, London (Author)

11. The Earl and Countess of Harewood with the Hon. Gerald Lascelles and his wife Angela at the Stoll Theatre, London, 1952

12. GLORIANA; Lord and Lady Harewood attending the run through of the opera Gloriana created to mark Queen Elizabeth's Coronation; 1953; Royal Opera House, Covent Garden, London, UK ; Photographer Roger Wood; Credit: Royal Ballet and Opera /ArenaPAL; www.arenapal.com

13. Marion Lascelles, Countess of Harewood with her two eldest sons, David and James, 1953

14. Marion with Maria Callas

15. Marion at the Royal Opera House Opera Ball

16. Visit to India 1958

17. Visit to India 1958

18. In Moscow for a Festival of British Musical Art organised by the British Council. Marion (R) sightseeing with

26. Marion and Jeremy Thorpe with Jeremy's young son, Rupert

27. Marion and Jeremy Thorpe with Rupert (Late 1970s)

28. Princess Margaret of Hesse, Jeremy Thorpe, Rupert Thorpe, Bettina Ehrlich and Marion Thorpe, at Curlews, Thorpeness, June 1976. Photograph: Nigel Luckhurst © Britten Pears Arts

29. Peter Pears seated left at rehearsal in Snape Maltings Concert Hall. His colleagues are Marion Thorpe and John Evans, with Donald Mitchell in the row behind, talking with Colin Matthews. 10-11 August 1985. Photograph: Nigel Luckhurst © Britten Pears Arts

30. Marion and Jeremy Thorpe, May 1994

ONE

ONE

Vienna

When, in spring 1938, Marion's father told her that they must leave Vienna, she was upset but not surprised. Even though she was a child, the sense of fear among Jewish neighbours and her father's work colleagues was palpable. She could see the quickened pace of Jews walking in the street, the nervous turn of the head to check whether there was anyone following, the relief of her mother when her father arrived home. Nazi hooligans were patrolling the district of Leopoldstadt in the city centre, where many Jews lived. Some socialist, Jewish and Zionist movements had united to form street patrols to take action against the swastika-wearing thugs who were attacking Jews. Nights were fraught with danger in the area. Her father was concerned for the future of his family in the heightened atmosphere of danger. It was time to go.

Young Marion would have to leave her comfortable home, her school friends, and her beloved piano. She would have to make new friends, learn a new language, change her plans for the future. But she was Daddy's girl and always would be. She was sure that he knew what was best. Eleven-year-old Marion packed the few things that the family were allowed to take into exile and trustingly accompanied her parents to a new life in London.

Marion's father did not discuss politics very much at home until the growing threat of Hitler came closer. But Marion remembered two dramatic and frightening occasions when she was a small child. In early 1934 there was a socialist workers' uprising and they could hear gunfire across the valley as the revolt was quashed. Later that year, 25 July, the Chancellor of Austria, Engelbert Dolfuss, was assassinated and her family, like many others, feared for the future of the country. Whether Erwin Stein fully realised the danger he faced in those early days is not clear. In 1933 his close friend, the composer Arnold Schoenberg, then working in Berlin had been contacted by some friends while he was holidaying in France to say that returning to Vienna could be dangerous. This warning came despite Schoenberg being technically no longer Jewish, having converted to Protestantism in 1898 and been baptised in Vienna. Heeding the advice from his friends in Germany to stay out of his country, he reconverted to Judaism whilst in Paris, thereby making both a religious and national-political statement. He immediately applied to emigrate, first to Britain, where he was refused, and then to the more-welcoming United States.

Erwin and Sophie, despite living and working in a reasonably prosperous part of the city, and not identifying with any extreme form of Judaism, must have known why their friend had left Berlin and would also be aware of the growing unrest in their own city. Although Erwin was ethnically a Jew, the family were Protestants by religion. But being a Protestant had not protected his friend Schoenberg and the latter's need to move to the US worried Erwin. Then working for music publisher Universal Edition in central Vienna, he started to put out feelers for similar jobs in other countries. Leslie Boosey, from a corresponding music publisher in England, Boosey and Hawkes came to Vienna to visit Universal Edition, and offered him an editorial job in London if he was forced to leave Vienna.

On March 11-13 1938 German troops invaded Austria. The Chancellor of Austria, Schuschnigg had attempted to keep Austria independent but his attempt had failed. "Just after lunch on that 11th March," writes George Newman in his memoir,[1] "the last day of independent Austria, Vienna fell silent. The city was waiting. The radio played patriotic music and it was announced that Schuschnigg would speak to the nation. No one seemed to be about in the streets. People were gathered round their radios for the broadcast. Schuschnigg told the people that he was yielding to a superior force and that he did not want bloodshed." There was such enthusiasm from the Austrians that Hitler annexed Austria the following day. By lunchtime on 12 March, practically every house in the centre of Vienna had a swastika flag flying. George, a Jewish boy just two years older than Marion, recalled how his father went with a sympathetic non-Jewish friend to collect a flag from the local police station. They hoped that by flying the huge Nazi banner that Jewish tenants of the flats would not be identified by the lack of such a flag. Austrians, now suddenly Germans, marched down the city streets to join thousands of their fellow citizens in Nazi celebration. The Steins did not see the military parades or welcoming crowds as they lived on the outskirts of the city. But, like all the other Viennese residents, they were glued to the wireless for news.

Prominent Jews, leading bankers, dentists, professors, doctors and lawyers were targeted and many of them left Vienna before they could be arrested. George Newman's uncle Robert, an outspoken banker, left immediately after the Chancellor Schuschnigg's broadcast. Twelve hours later, on the first morning of the Anschluss, two Gestapo men rang the bell at his flat demanding "Wo ist der Jude Neumann." Thankfully they were too late. George was told that he and his mother were leaving Vienna at lunchtime on Monday 14 March. At two o'clock that afternoon, clutching a small suitcase and his precious violin, he said goodbye to his father on the station platform. Czechoslovakia, Hungary and Italy had either closed their borders or made travel hazardous, but Switzerland was still open without an entry visa. Mother and son arrived in Zurich late at night, travelled on through France and then crossed the channel into England. Many years after the war, the musical George would become a young colleague of Erwin in London.

Marion's father did not react immediately to the dangers to Jews in Vienna. Perhaps he felt that working in music publishing he would not be seen as a threat to the Nazis or that having a non-Jewish wife and claiming to be a Protestant, the family was safe. However, over the spring and summer of 1938, life for the family became increasingly hard.

A controlled plebiscite of April 10 gave 99.7 percent approval to Austria becoming part of Germany. Many of those voting could not have known how this Anschluss, or political union, would impact on their lives. Once in power the Nazis applied German anti-Jewish legislation to Austria. Jews were excluded from all economic, social and cultural life. Gestapo headquarters were set up in every area. Officials closed Jewish community offices and sent board members to Dachau concentration camp. Jewish owned businesses were closed or confiscated. Erwin's workplace Universal Edition was Aryanised. Although his bosses were apologetic, there was no choice. There was no further place for him there.

Children too were not immune to these changes. The young Marion and her Jewish friend Susi had long, grown-up discussions about the political situation in their country and they knew that life was changing. Each morning at school, class began with "Heil Hitler" and the Nazi salute. The Jewish girls were put on one side of the class. Marion was thought to be Aryan so she and Susi were separated. A Nazi supporting girl accused her of being friendly with 'that Jewish girl Susi', and Marion was proud to insist that Susi was her friend and always would be. When her school broke up that year, Marion had a good report – but the heading to the document was no longer Republik Osterreich but rather Deutches Reich. She was officially a German child.

In early1938, the Steins were living in an apartment in a large house on the outskirts of Vienna in Potzleinsdorf, an area where many professional people had their homes. Very like Hampstead as Marion remembered. There were just three large apartments in the building, a large garden for the tenants and a view across the vineyards of Grinzing, up to the Kahlenberg mountain, a popular beauty spot. Her closest friends were Susi, the daughter of the architect who had designed the building and another Susi, who lived in a beautiful 'Bauhaus' dwelling up the road. Marion's life was good. But after the Anschluss, change came quickly. It was a shock to Marion to find her family targeted by the Nazis as both her parents, although not religious, claimed to be Protestant. Sophie, her mother was German and Marion was not at all aware of her Jewish background. But the Germans were aware. To make room for a German officer and his family, the Nazis turned the Steins out of their flat and relocated them to a small apartment next door. The son of Marion's neighbours was beaten up by Nazi thugs and a distinguished Jewish doctor who lived in the same house had his car taken away from him, effectively preventing him from doing his job. Very bravely, Sophie went to the authorities and complained vigorously about the treatment of their Jewish neighbours. In the autumn of 1938, after Marion's family had left Vienna and when the major deportations and persecutions had started, they heard that the Gestapo had been to their old flat looking for "that loud-mouthed German woman."

In this tense atmosphere, a mass migration of Viennese Jews began. Any Jewish and half-Jewish families who had the means got out of Austria as fast as they could. Erwin Stein, his wife Sophie and his daughter Marion were all in danger. He and many of his extended family planned their escape.

Just over eleven years earlier, on October 18 1926, Erwin Stein and his wife Sophie had welcomed their new-born daughter to Vienna with an impressive list of first names, Maria Donata Nanetta Paulina Gustava Erwina Wilhelmina. This long list indicated perhaps, a liking by her parents of both the Austrian and the royal tradition of giving children many names and was, unknowingly, a foretaste of things to come. The name Maria Donata, gift of God, reflected the happy surprise of her parents who had not expected Sophie to bear another child. The last five names honoured the baby's two grandmothers and three step and half-brothers. Her 17- year-old half-brother Karl Gustav, known as Kagu, thought that Maria Donata was too high-falutin a name for a small girl and amalgamated them into Marion, a name she kept for the rest of her life.

Her parents were by no means royal. Her father Erwin Stein was a conductor and music editor, having in his younger days been part of composer Schoenberg's circle in Vienna and a great supporter of Mahler. He was ethnically Jewish but his family had converted to Protestantism and no longer practised the Jewish faith. Born in 1885 in Vienna where his family ran a publishing house, he was aged forty and relatively newly married when his only child, Marion, was born. Erwin's wife Sophie Bachman was a little older than her husband and forty-three when Marion was born, a welcome daughter for the family. She was German-born and a Protestant, the daughter of a Lutheran pastor in Mecklenburg-Strelitz, at that time one of Germany's smaller, grand ducal states. On marriage to a civil servant, a widower with two small sons, Erwin and Willie, she moved to Darmstadt with her new family and had another son, Kagu. Through her husband's position, she became involved in the life of the court and formed a link with a lady-in-waiting who was with the Hesse family. Many years later, when Prince Ludwig (Lu) of Hesse and his Scottish wife, Peg, contacted Sophie, the link would lead to friendships within Marion's musical circle.

The time just after the end of World War 1 was one of depression and hyper-inflation in Germany; many people felt unable to cope with their changed fortunes. Sophie's husband died. It is believed he committed suicide although Sophie did not talk about it. He left her with three young sons, no money and a large house in Darmstadt. To survive, she took in lodgers. When her niece Maria heard that a young visiting orchestral conductor needed somewhere to stay, she recommended him to Sophie. The relationship for the widowed Sophie and bachelor Erwin developed quickly, consolidated by her nursing him when he hurt his knee badly. They married and moved, soon after their marriage in 1924, back to Vienna, the musical centre of Austria. Sophie was plunged into a totally different world than that of Darmstadt, that of the most 'avant-garde' musical life of the period, the Schoenberg circle.

The couple made an unusual pair, very different in both looks and temperament. The diminutive, chubby Erwin, barely five feet tall was busy and energetic, Marion's mother, the tall blonde Sophie Bachman 'seemed to float thro life- all Viennese charm'[2] But she was a strong woman and when necessary, she asserted herself. Marion inherited her dark good looks from her father, her height from Sophie, and elements of her character from both.

Now a family man, Erwin worked as an editor for the Viennese publishing house Universal Edition at Karlsplatz 6, where he continued to develop his interest in modern music. A well-respected music teacher and conductor, Stein also wrote articles about the music and composers whose work he admired. As a young man, Erwin had studied with Arnold Schoenberg, the Vienna-born music theorist, teacher, writer, and painter. Schoenberg was one of the most influential composers of the 20th century and the leader of the so-called Second Viennese School, which Marion said was her father's circle. Erwin, a great enthusiast for the composer's music, was a key assistant in organizing the Society for Private Musical Performances and he and Schoenberg became friends. And in 1924 it was to Stein that Schoenberg entrusted the task of writing a first article – Neue Formprinzipien ('New Formal Principles') – on a subject that was soon to be explicitly formulated as 'twelve-tone technique'. Erwin continued to write, teach and conduct. The Steins quickly became well-established and influential characters in the musical and cultural life of the city.

As she grew up in Vienna Marion was very aware of the role that music would play in her life. Her first memories were of a flat in the Mossengasse, listening to her father accompany a singer, and later standing in front of a mirror copying the song she had been singing. "bald grass ich am Neckaar, bald grass ich am Rhein" (Now I reap by the Neckar, now I reap by the Rhine). Later she said that she had not realised then that it was rather a risqué song. Many of her father's friends were musicians and she grew up in a musical world. His closest friend was composer Alban Berg, 'Onkel Alban', who called Marion his little hazel-nut because of her dark eyes and skin. Alban was a very tall man and rather intimidating to a small girl. Marion remembered that after he died, at only fifty years old on Christmas Eve 1935, their maid, doing the spring clean, found a full ashtray on top of a cupboard, one that only Alban could reach.

When she was about four, the family moved into her grandfather's flat above the family publishing house, Manz Verlag am Kohlmarkt, in central Vienna. Other members of the family lived there too. Soon, however, her parents found their own apartment in a new house on the outskirts of Vienna.

It was a very happy childhood. She celebrated St Nicholas day with children of a Dutch banker who lived nearby. Nikolo, dressed like father Christmas brought presents to the children who waited expectantly for him to arrive on a beautiful white horse. Other friends were three boys from the Illitch family who lived in a splendid house with a pool, tea house and playground, a bowling alley and a small theatre. She went skating with Ivan, one of the Illitch boys of her own age. His family too were part Jewish and later emigrated to America.

A major event in her young life, etched in Marion's memory, was the visit to a peasant family in Burgenland, close the Hungarian border. The family maid, Emma, came from that area and one year she took Marion with her. The details were still very clear when many years later, Marion wrote about that visit. She and Emma travelled from the station in an ox cart and she slept with all the other women and girls in one bedroom. The family all dressed in peasant costume. There was no water which had to be brought from a well, no electricity and Marion had to wash in a basin. She joined in the haymaking, collected eggs from the chickens and went to market. Being a peasant girl was a wonderful experience for a town girl and Marion loved it.

Christmas was very special in Austria. Every evening in Advent Marion's father would play carols and she would open a window of her little paper advent house. Every night too there would be a silver 'hair' (very fine silver tinsel) left by her bedside to say that the Christ Child had passed in the night. But unlike in England, the big celebration in Austria was on Christmas Eve when the tall tree would be lit by real candles and covered in chocolates. Presents, traditionally not wrapped, would be laid out on a table. The family sat down to a traditional supper of carp.

From the age of eight, Marion was taken to the opera. It was a great treat and opera continued to play a large part in her life. She recorded that her first visit was to *Hansel and Gretel* and her father chose what he thought were other morally suitable operas for her to see. The libretto had to be appropriate. She saw *The Magic Flute, The Bartered bride* and *The Flying Dutchman* which were deemed not to be 'naughty', but she had to wait to see the more risqué stories of *Figaro, Don Giovanni, Carmen* and *La Boheme* until she was older. She developed a particular love for Mozart and enthusiastically took to the piano when her father arranged lessons, although she did not think that she made much progress at the time. She learned to read music quickly and would listen to the radio, following the score with her father. Quite an active child, Marion learned ballet and to skate. She was taken to the local ice rink in the centre of the town by her mother who was a stately skater.

Many summer holidays were spent with aunt Hedwig, her mother's sister, in Auerbach, Hessen. The large house in the village accommodated three generations of the family for holidays and Marion played with her cousin's daughter Carmen, who was three years older than her. One year, Carmen gave Marion a rather garbled account of the facts of life; Marion didn't believe her until much later. She remembered only two different holidays with her parents: one to Italy when she was small and another to the Salzkammergut by the lake of Grundlsee. There she learned to swim.

Back in Vienna, Marion went first to the local primary school and then at nine to the Gymnasium. She and Susi Rezck travelled by bus unless Susi's father, a doctor, gave them a lift in his car. This was a treat as few people in Erwin's circle had cars. Marion did well at school. She enjoyed learning and got top marks. Things were going well. But in the wider world, things were changing fast and these changes would affect her family along with many of their friends and neighbours.

Despite the rumblings of change in the early 1930s, musical life was still very important to the Viennese and in 1934, a visitor arrived in the city; one who would have a major effect on the Stein family's life, although at that time there was no hint of such a relationship to come. Benjamin Britten, the talented young British composer, not yet twenty-one, was on a six-week cultural tour of Europe, paid for by a music scholarship. His mother, recently bereaved, accompanied her son.

Already some of Britten's compositions were receiving wider attention outside music school circles; his *Phantasy* quartet was broadcast by the BBC in February 1933 and *A Boy was Born*, a set of choral variations was written that year and performed the following year by the BBC singers. In April 1934 he visited Florence where his *Phantasy* oboe quartet was performed again, his first overseas performance. The trip to Europe in autumn that year was a chance to visit Basle, Salzburg, Munich, Paris, and also Vienna, where Britten hoped to meet prominent musical figures. He was by this time particularly interested in the music of Stravinsky, Shostakovich and Mahler and had wanted to study in Vienna with Alban Berg. But the plan had come to nothing as his parents and the staff at the Royal College of Music had dissuaded him; they thought Berg 'not a good influence'.

He was already aware of Erwin Stein although, at the time of his visit, he probably did not know how important a part Stein played in the musical life of the city. Four years earlier, in his diary entry for Monday 7 April 1930[3], the sixteen-year-old schoolboy, Benjamin Britten, refers to a visit to a friend's house to hear a 'marvellous Schonberg concert on the Billison's wireless'. He commented that he enjoyed Arnold Schoenberg's *Pierrot Lunaire* the most. 'I thought it most beautiful. It was of course perfectly done.' The concert was a BBC concert of contemporary music 'held privately' at the Central Hall Westminster. The Vienna Pierrot Luminaire Ensemble was conducted by Erwin Stein.

On 8 November 1934 Britten wrote to his close friend Grace Williams from the Hotel Regina in Vienna. Britten knew that she too had visited the city on a travelling scholarship in 1930 and studied with Egon Wellesz. Ben was very impressed with Vienna's people and music. He wrote to Grace, 'I met a very nice man from the Universal Edition – introduction from Foss – one Dr. Heinsheimer. I had a long talk with him, in broken English and German, and he has kept some of my stuff to show to Erwin Stein whom I am to meet on Saturday."[4] Dr Hans Heinsheimer was a German and head of the opera department of Universal Edition, the great Viennese Publishing house at the time Britten was visiting Vienna. It was also the workplace of Erwin Stein. Britten met 'Dr Stein', as he referred to Erwin, on 10 November and then again, just over a week later, at a concert. He would have had no idea that this man would later be a person to have a major effect on his career and his personal relationships. He did not meet the rest of the Stein family on that visit, but the eight-year-old Marion too would later become a very important part of his life.

At 21 years old in 1934, and practising only basic schoolboy German which was useful later in his friendship with the Russian cellist, Mstislav Rostropovich and the composer Dmitri Shostakovich, Britten was just dimly aware of the growing tensions in Vienna. He mentions in his letter to his friend Grace Williams that "the Viennese themselves are lovely people.... I think that they are the kindest, cheerfulest (sic) people I have ever met. And they are going through pretty dreadful times too, but it doesn't seem so by their expressions."[5] Despite recognising that something was amiss, he could not know that four years later, there would be much more dreadful times for Viennese Jews. And that life would change dramatically for the Stein family.

In the spring of 1938, Vienna became the centre of Jewish emigration from Austria. Those wanting to leave had to stand in long lines waiting for the exit visas and other documentation that were needed to leave the country. They had to pay an exorbitant exit fee and register all of their immovable, and most of their movable property which was confiscated before they left. During the course of Aryanization, Erwin Stein was forced to sell his stockholdings in Universal Edition. The company bowed to pressure, was Nazified, and all their many Jewish employees lost their jobs. As an additional insult to his musicality, Erwin was also forbidden to publish any more of his writings. However, his old employers gave Erwin a testimony to take with him to his new life. They wrote that he had worked for Universal Edition from 1924 to 38, that he was so well-known in the musical world that his capability spoke for itself. They stressed the importance of his work for them, and stated that under his leadership the orchestral part of the company had greatly increased, and that he had a good knowledge of the music of many countries. They ended with a heartfelt "Best wishes go with Mr Erwin Stein for his future career."

The emigrees scattered to any country where they hoped to be safe from the Nazis, many to the US and the UK. 130,000 left Austria during this time, of whom

30,000 headed for the US. Erwin chose to go into exile in London. His wife Sophie had to leave her three adult sons behind, all of whom were German. She did not know what would become of them. Marion's mother must have been particularly conflicted at the thought of leaving her sons and her homeland. Marion was leaving her half-brother Kagu behind too. Suddenly she was an only child. While Erwin went directly to London, Sophie and Marion decided to visit relations to say goodbye. They wanted to go to Auerbach where Aunt Hedwig had a house and where Marion had spent every summer holiday. However much to the disgust of Sophie and Marion, the family decided that because Marion was half-Jewish, they would be too exposed in the small town and that this would reflect unfortunately on the resident family. So, Sophie and her daughter stayed in a pension in Berlin over Marion's twelfth birthday and were visited by Aunt Hedwig, Maria and Kagu. who then drove them to Strelitz, Sophie's birthplace. The disenchanted mother and daughter left Germany for London in October. Arriving at Liverpool Street Station they were welcomed by Erwin and two second cousins of Sophie who were British residents. One of these cousins was 'Aunt' 'Laura, the widow of a Pre Raphaelite artist, Roland Aning-Bell, herself a painter with a studio in Melbury Road, Holland Park.

Twelve-year-old Marion had been uprooted from all she had known; the life of a schoolgirl and promising pianist, her comfortable musical and well-connected family. Suddenly the family were in exile, comparatively poor and the future was uncertain. England was a strange country with an unfamiliar language.

However, they were safe. They were among the lucky ones who had been able to leave what had been Austria. They reached the UK just in time. Just eight months after Hitler's triumphal entry into Vienna, life for Vienna's remaining Jewish community took an even more dramatic turn. The anti-Jewish pogrom known as 'Kristallnacht' or 'the Night of Broken Glass' was launched on 9–10 November. In Vienna, as in other towns and cities in Germany and Austria, Nazi hit squads torched synagogues, together with shops and businesses owned by Jews. Most synagogues and prayer houses in Vienna were destroyed. Over 6000 Jews were arrested in this one night; the majority were deported to the Dachau concentration camp in the following days. The antisemitic and racist Nuremberg laws, introduced in Germany in 1935, were applied in Austria from May 1938 and reinforced with innumerable decrees. Jews were gradually robbed of their freedoms, were blocked from almost all professions, were shut out of schools and universities. On 1 September 1941, Reinhard Heydrich decreed that all Jews in the Reich or annexed territories six years of age or older were to wear the Yellow Badge, a yellow star of David on a black background to be worn on the chest, with the word "Jew" inscribed. The badge was intended not only to stigmatize and humiliate the Jews but also to identify them when Nazi squads were rounding them up for deportation to the concentration camps.

As the Steins began their new life in London, they realised that they would never see many of their friends, neighbours and colleagues again.

TWO

A New Life

L ondon was not as unfamiliar or as unwelcoming as it could have been for Marion's family.

Her father Erwin found somewhere for the family to live; first a flat in Belsize Park and later one in Cornwall Gardens, South Kensington. He quickly took up the job as an editor at Boosey and Hawkes, Britain's principal music publisher, a role which he had been offered by Leslie Boosey some years before. As early as 1923, Ralph Hawkes, the Managing Director of Hawkes and Sons, which merged with Boosey and Co in 1930, had travelled to Vienna and negotiated the sole agency for Universal Edition with the copyrights of such major composers as Schoenberg, Bartok, Mahler, Webern and Kodaly.[6] Erwin's knowledge and love of such composers made him a welcome addition to Hawkes's staff. Boosey and Hawkes took the opportunity of employing many of Universal Edition's executives, many of them Jewish, and the influx facilitated the publisher's fast development as a champion of modern music. Many of Erwin's colleagues from Vienna, composers and publishing figures had also found a home in London. These included the composers Zoltán Kodaly, Béla Bartok and Leopold Spinner and Czech-born Ernst Roth, head of publications at Universal Editions. Roth eventually became the general manager at Boosey and Hawkes and, after the war, gave the young George Newman, also a refugee from Vienna, a job in the company, where he worked with Erwin. By 1939 there were plenty of old friends of the Steins in London. Those who had scattered to various parts of the world after the Anschluss kept in touch by letter and many visited after the war. Cousin Marie, the daughter of Sophie's sister who had moved to Paris after the Anschluss, lived with the Steins in London for some time in the 1940s and Aunt Paula, her father's eldest sister, a rather eccentric woman, moved to Ceylon (now Sri Lanka) in 1938 as a teacher. She continued to send advice about Theosophy and personal horoscopes to Marion until she died in 1952.

Marion had turned 12 in October 1938 while she and her mother were in Berlin, so it was important now to find her a good school. She attended a Catholic school run by nuns for a short time while she and her mother searched, unsuccessfully for some time, for a school which would take a young refugee with hardly any English. Marion was so angry with the Germans and what had happened to her country that she refused to speak German, even at home. It must have been a very difficult time for her and for her parents. Help came in the form of new friends, the Brennan family whose two girls, Anne and Lydia attended Kensington Girls School and who suggested that the Steins should try to place Marion there. Miss Wordsworth, the headmistress agreed to take Marion into the school at a reduced rate. This would still be too much for Erwin on £6 per week, but more help came when Ralph Hawkes, the head of Boosey and Hawkes offered to cover the fees.

In early 1939, Marion, horrified that she had to wear a school uniform, an unbecoming set of a white blouse, gym tunic, black knickers, thick stockings and a 'hideous pot-shaped hat', started her new school life at Kensington High School. She spoke very little English and refused to speak much until she grew more confident. But she was determined that this was her new life and she would not look back to Vienna. This attitude stayed with her throughout her life; she accepted situations as they were and moved on without too obvious regret. Help to learn the new language came when the headmistress suggested that she spend some time with another pupil, the daughter of the English mistress. Marion's English improved rapidly. As an adult there was no trace of a Viennese accent, but there was just a very occasional trace of German grammar; a shift of verb or the use of a different idiom.

By the end of the summer term 1939 she was doing so well that her report referred to her 'excellent progress', in fact so well that in the autumn she was awarded a scholarship to cover her fees. And Erwin was sent a refund for those he had already paid for that term. Yet more change came when war broke out in 1939. London was considered too dangerous for the girls and the school was evacuated to Oxford and amalgamated with Oxford High School with a new headmistress, Miss Burke. Some of the girls were billeted with local families but Sophie and Marion took rooms in the Northern Gardens area of Oxford, Erwin visiting as often as he could from his work in London. In a press article in 1949, Miss Burke remembered that time ten years earlier when Marion, a happy, clever and charming child, came to Oxford with her dark hair in two plaits. Many of the girls remained in Oxford at the Christmas of 1939 so Miss Burke made it her business to visit each one. Marion's home was her last call. As a memory of Vienna, there was a Christmas tree in the sitting room and Sophie, Erwin, Marion and Miss Burke had a small party. "It was the happiest Christmas night I ever remember," said Miss Burke. But all the girls missed London, and very soon the school returned to London and stayed there throughout the bombing. Marion had a reminder that the war could still be dangerous to her when the school at Lytham House in Kensington was destroyed by a bomb in 1941. It was relocated to Phillimore Gardens, adjacent to Holland Park, slightly nearer to Marion's home. The move was supposedly a temporary measure, but the school stayed there until 1948.

Marion was bright. By summer 1940, only a year after arriving at the school with very little English she was achieving high marks in the lower IV class, she even took top place in History, Science, Algebra, Geometry and Latin and fourth place was her lowest. However, Physical Education was never a strong point. Her teacher commented that Marion found it difficult to shift her weight to get over the vaulting horse! But she participated well in games.

Erwin had settled well into the culture of Boosey and Hawkes and in 1939, just a year after his arrival with the publisher, he was instrumental in founding Tempo, the modern music journal. This began as the house newsletter of Boosey and Hawkes but became a more independent publication and is still published today by Cambridge University Press. Erwin's focus was mainly on Schoenberg and Mahler but by the time World War II broke out in September 1939, Boosey and Hawkes had signed Benjamin Britten, to whom Erwin Stein later became a friend, close supporter and confidant.

Earlier that year Marion had met her father's friend Britten for the first time. The composer's impassioned anti-war *Ballad of the Heroes*, published by Boosey and Hawkes, was premiered on the 5 April 1939 at the Queen's Hall in London as part of a Festival of Music for the People, conducted by Constant Lambert. Marion was now considered old enough to go to concerts and she was introduced to Benjamin by her father who had met the composer in Vienna five years earlier. Marion's Viennese curtsey charmed Britten. On her part, she was instantly attracted to the good-looking twenty-five-year-old and the adolescent Marion duly fell in love. In later years a friend commented that Marion's friendship with Britten was a love affair that could never have been. She would not have realised at that time that his preferences were for men. However, that meeting was the beginning of a friendship that would become a close one and would last for the composer's lifetime.

The professional relationship between Erwin Stein and Britten had to be a distant one in the early war years. Benjamin Britten and his new lover Peter Pears left for the US in April 1939 via Quebec, following the example of two of their friends, the poet W.H. Auden and the prose writer Christopher Isherwood. There were various reasons for the move: both Britten and Pears were pacifists and decried the war, but also their friends were in the US and Frank Bridge, Britten's friend and early teacher had enjoyed success there. Britten's work had received criticism in the British music press before 1939 and this seemingly unpatriotic move away from Britain only increased the hostility towards Britten and Pears. Erwin however, remained a supporter of his protégé, and letters travelled between the UK and Britten in the US throughout the war.

From Quebec, Britten and Pears moved on to New York and started to live with the Mayers, Dr William Mayers, a psychiatrist, his wife. Elizabeth and their family. Elizabeth, a German born translator and editor used her homes in Long Island as salons for visiting writers and musicians and welcomed the composer and singer wholeheartedly. Whilst it would perhaps be too fanciful to say that Britten saw in Elizabeth a replacement for his mother, who had died only two years previously, he was susceptible to her warmth of welcome. Although he was finally liberated from his mother's dominating influence, he grieved for her, feeling partly responsible for her death which had occurred when she had been in London looking after Ben and his sister Beth when they had pneumonia. Elizabeth Mayer did become very close to Ben. He enjoyed the warmth of the environment in Long Island, and this may have influenced the need in him to live later in a house with a family atmosphere. When he returned to London later in the war, he sought to share his home with others. The Stein family were to make him welcome and to some extent, replace the Meyers. Pears too considered the Steins as almost 'second Mayers.'

Although London was very much home for the Steins and Marion was settled at school, there were complications. Erwin, one of some 70,000 resident Germans and Austrians in the UK, was classed as an enemy alien. Such registered enemy aliens were examined by around 120 internment tribunals, many in London where large number of German and Austrians lived. They were classified into three categories. Aliens in the A category were thought to be a security risk and would be interned, the Bs would be exempt from internment but be subject to restrictions, and those in category C, would be exempt from both internment and restriction. Most Jewish refugees from Austria were considered to be in category C. So, in 1939 and early 1940, except for the irritation of attending a tribunal, life went on for Erwin as usual and he was free to live and work in London.

However, these were the early days of the war, a time of heightened paranoia, and both the wartime government and the public started to believe that the risk of a German invasion was high. The suspicion grew, unfounded or not, that some of the emigres who had escaped from persecution might be enemy spies. The decision was made to intern them all in camps. In retrospect it seems a strange policy to include the Jewish emigres in this round-up, the very people who were probably the strongest enemies of Hitler. But many civilians who were born in enemy countries were either transported or were sent to internment camps in Britain. Those, like the Steins, who had fled from what had been Austria, were technically Germans. In May 1940, regardless of their category classification, many Germans and Austrians resident in the Southern strip of England, including Marion's father, found themselves sent many miles away from their families into internment camps.

Like many other "enemy aliens" Erwin was not transported but was interned. A sad little note from him to Sophie has only six words. 'I am interned. I am well.' He was only allowed a short message, nevertheless his family were glad to hear from him. On 28 June 1940 he writes, 'I am at Kempton Park racecourse Internment camp. I am well. I will let you know my permanent address soon, Erwin.' The 'permanent' address during his internment was to be Central Camp, House 12, Douglas, Isle of Man. In reports about his time on the island, some writers have assumed that Erwin was sent to Hutchinson Camp, because it housed many Austrians, and a high proportion of Jewish and anti-Nazi men. It was also known as "the artists' camp" as it contained many of those connected with the Arts. The musical internees made music there however they could, and although printed material was banned, those with access to instruments gave recitals from memory. However, Erwin had no such luck. Central Camp which opened in June 1940 consisted of a square block of hotels from Empress Drive to Castle Drive. Many of the houses in the town, which were used as boarding houses for holiday visitors before the war were now requisitioned for the internees. Some of the landladies stayed and catered for the internees rather than holiday makers. The total of 34 properties held about 2,000 internees and like the other camps it was surrounded by a barbed wire fence to prevent escapes. It closed after a year and became H.M.S Valkyrie II, and was used to train signalmen for the D-Day landings.

Many letters to Erwin from his family and friends exist and his letters to them. Post was sometime held up which caused anxiety, and every letter was opened at the office of The Chief Postal Censor-Liverpool. Erwin chafed against his life in the camp. "You can imagine how I hate it here, the more so as it is so unnecessary." In July 1940 he is concerned about what is happening to his wife and child back in London without him. He writes in English and Sophie does too although she probably needed some help from Marion. Writing in German would probably have caused delays at the censors. "My dearest, I am still without any letter from you and you can imagine how I am longing for news from you .... I have no idea how your financial position is, and what is going to be with the school, the flat, the piano etc." In another letter he says he would have liked to hear a speech by Churchill and tells his family about the people at the camp. "There are not many people to get on with here but some are very nice - e.g. a professor from Karlsruhe with whom I am on good terms.... I shall be happy to tell you the many queer stories that happen hear (sic) out of the fact that so many dissimilar people from all classes, ages and districts are compelled to live together."

Marion writes often to Erwin, her "dearest Daddy," chatty letters that tell him all about her life and what she is doing at school. In late July 1940 she writes to tell him all about her end of year school report and copies it out meticulously for him, even including her own age and the average age of the class. She has received two cups of which she is 'terribly proud,' the Junior Roberts Cup for Diving and the Junior Speed Cup (swimming). Her mother gave her 2 shillings and sixpence for such a good report and Aunt Laura '1 bob'. On 30 September 1940 she tells him that her mother and she are going to move from 12 Southwell Gardens to 'a very elegant and nice flat quite near, 100 Cornwall Gardens, just round the corner from here.' The brother of a friend was going to Oxford and he was offering Marion and Sophie his flat for £1.1s a week (about £42 today). A very generous offer. And there was a piano although she would miss 'the Steinway.' She tells her father that she has to write an essay for school about 'A Raidy Day'. She tells him what she had written. She says that all the girls have to go to the air raid shelter mid lesson, taking their books with them There is the 'all clear' for break and then it's down again to the shelters when the siren sounds at lunchtime. They play 'murders' in the playtime after lunch in the shelter. Marion tells her father about the subjects she intends to choose for her General Schools exam. "Already I'm terribly worried about it and I have 2 more years to go." She won't take biology, she tells him, she hates it. She signs off her letter, "well I must quickly post this letter before Hitler pays us another visit. Much love and affection and millions of xxx, Yours, Marion."

Erwin spent a relatively peaceful although frustrating few months in the Isle of Man and managed to continue some of his work from the camp. A letter from him to Mr Leslie (a colleague at Boosey and Hawkes) sent detailed instructions about how a score, a Handel Suite, should be changed before publication, and suggested some details should be checked by Beecham.[7] The accompanying letter suggested that good friends were trying to secure his release. It ends:

"I was glad to receive your letter of 16th July and hope Mrs Stein thanked you for it and expressed my apology for not answering – you know we are very restricted in writing. We now get papers regularly. So I am quite aware of the present situation which seems to develop satisfactorily, thanks to the R.A.F. Mrs Stein told me that you are very hopeful about my release. This is a great consolation and thank you very much for your endeavours, and all your help. With kindest regards, Yours sincerely, Erwin Stein"

Although they were not without Erwin for too many months, it was a difficult time for Sophie and Marion. They were reduced to living in their flat on an allowance from Boosey and Hawkes of £3 a week, half Erwin's normal salary, with no knowledge of when Erwin would return.

He was soon back in London but despite his comparative freedom he still, like other refugees, continued to register as an enemy alien, an irritation to him. Once at home, Erwin returned to his job at Boosey and Hawkes and the family widened their social circle through music. It was, however, a very upsetting time for Marion's mother Sophie who must have worked hard to cope with her new life. She was worried about her three sons that she had left behind and who were now citizens of an enemy country. She was especially concerned for her youngest son Kagu, Marion's half-brother, who was a German test pilot. By a circuitous route, she eventually discovered that he had been killed in an air crash although not in combat. Willie, the second of her stepsons, who lived and worked in Java, also died at the beginning of the war. When the Japanese were about to occupy Indonesia, a Dutch colony, the Dutch interned all Germans and shipped them to India. The boat that Willie was on sank with no survivors.

Erwin, the eldest step son, the only one to survive, was captured near the end of the war and spent time in a Russian prisoner of war camp. Scarred by his experiences there, he did manage to visit his mother post-war. It must have been particularly hard for Sophie that her grief for what were at that time, the enemies of her adopted country, had to be borne privately and stoically, and there were times when she was, understandably, depressed. She was a very emotional woman, who could cry with laughter and then be down in the dumps, and this was not always easy for her family to live with. But somehow she managed to cope with the sad events in her life as the war progressed. Marion, although still in her teens, was less emotional than her mother and a great support to her. But Marion too must have been upset at the loss of her siblings. Her step brothers were much older than her and had left home by the time she was born but Kagu had been a part of her younger life in Vienna, and was an affectionate half-brother to his young sister.

The government was keen to maintain the morale of both those fighting and those at home and wartime was, unexpectedly, a good time to hear music. There were concerts and recitals in London and in the provinces. Looking back many years later, Marion was surprised how life seemed to carry on quite normally. Apart from having to sleep in the basement cellars of the flat in Cornwall Gardens during bombing raids, and needing to carry a gas-mask at all times, her teenage years continued as before. Marion enjoyed taking her turn in fire-watching shifts with adults. She attended a lot of concerts in the war years. She queued for the Promenade Concerts in the Albert Hall where they had moved after the bombing of the Queen's Hall. Standing to hear the music she got to know the classical repertoire. Her father was involved with the Boosey and Hawkes concerts in the Wigmore Hall, where works published largely by them were performed. Many of the first performances of Benjamin Britten were heard there. Marion enthusiastically supported her friend and house mate Ben's music. There were concerts to enjoy at the National Gallery too. The gallery had been cleared of pictures for safe storage and the room converted to a chamber music venue. The curator Kenneth Clark and pianist Myra Hess founded a series of lunchtime concerts which were attended by anyone lucky enough to be in London at midday. Many tired workers, their nights broken by bombing, gained new energy from the music. Marion remembered that one recital by Britten and Pears continued undisturbed as a loud explosion was heard nearby.

Britten and Pears had returned to Britain on 16 March 1942. Although their trip to the United was intended to be for only a few months when they had left Britain, it was two and a half years before the pair arrived back home. On arriving in England Britten and Pears both applied for recognition as conscientious objectors. This was granted on condition they gave recitals under the auspices of the Council for the Encouragement of Music and the Arts. Britten was still one of Boosey and Hawkes's composers and in 1943 Britten wrote to Erwin from the Grove Fever

Hospital[8] where he had been sent after a bad attack of measles. He told Erwin that he was not allowed to work until the end of April. He had listened to one of his works on a nurse's radio and asked Erwin for his comments about that score and his opinions about a potential ballet for Frederic Ashton. The close professional relationship between Erwin and Britten was re-established, and soon it became one which embraced Sophie and Marion too. This friendship was part of the musical thread that intricately linked all the stages of Marion's life. Already she was becoming a competent pianist and took every opportunity to listen to and learn about music. She continued to do well at school and passed her 'O' level exams with flying colours. As a result, she gained a scholarship to stay on to study for A levels, Music, History and German. Marion's traumatic departure from her home in Austria which had led to her aversion to her original language was now less painful and she was able to choose German as one of her subjects for A level. Having studied the piano at school and done well, she decided to work towards a career as a professional pianist. Her teacher at school Miss Mountfort, a member of the Bach choir was a very good teacher even though, Marion recalled later, she didn't really like any music after Brahms, and possibly Elgar. She disapproved of Marion's 'modern music' connections. "None of that modern stuff like Britten and God forbid Schoenberg and Berg." In the summer of 1944, when Marion left school to pursue her new career, a final school report accompanied her.

"Marion's work has reached a high standard in all subjects and, in spite of enemy action, I hope to see this reflected in her Higher Certificate Results. Marion has been a helpful and very pleasant member of the school. I shall watch her career with great interest and I wish her every success in the future."

I am sure her headmistress Miss Burke was very surprised at how soon her former pupil's 'career' took off in directions unimaginable by both at the time.

THREE

Moving On

In November 1944, the Stein's London home was destroyed. The flat above had caught fire and water poured through the ceiling below. Their home was uninhabitable. Thankfully the only handwritten manuscript of Benjamin Britten's new opera, *Peter Grimes*, temporarily in Erwin's possession, miraculously escaped a soaking. Britten's first concern was for his manuscript which in those days would have been the only copy. "Erwin's flat has been drenched as the house caught fire but luckily the P.G. score is safe"[9] he wrote to Pears. But then his concern was for the Steins. Very generously he and Pears invited the homeless family to share their maisonette at 45A St John's Wood High Street and Erwin, Sophie and Marion moved in. John Lindsay, the pianist, a friend of Britten's in the 1940s, described life in the house.[10] Sophie Stein ran the place with style, giving orders to the live-in housekeeper who cost the household £182 a year in wages. Meals were 'ordered affairs,' sometimes waited upon by Marion. She was still a schoolgirl but already a serious pianist, practising long hours. He father Erwin "while not overseeing Boosey and Hawkes's growing catalogue, gave lessons and consultations at home, often enough helping decode works by his teacher Schoenberg."

The house became a real home to this extended musical family. Winifred Roberts, the violinist and a good friend of Benjamin Britten, reported 'a jolly party' to celebrate Stein's 60th birthday, November 7, 1945. Britten, Pears and Ronnie Duncan played and sang and Marion and Winifred played a piano duet.[11]

The war, at least in Europe, had ended a few months previously. On V-E (Victory in Europe) day, 7 May 1945 there was great excitement at seeing London lit up once more as Marion and her family watched from Hampstead Heath. Having left school the previous year she was now studying the piano seriously, at first at the Royal College of Music. A friend of Benjamin Britten who espoused modern music, the pianist Clifford Curzon, encouraged her towards a career as a pianist and became a good mentor; she recalls that she could ring him and discuss details such as how to finger a Mozart passage. Marion, now living with Britten and Pears was aware of all the preparations for the premiere of Britten's first real opera,[12] *Peter Grimes* on June 7 1945 at the Sadlers Wells Theatre. She was very excited and was at close quarters for rehearsals and preparation. Marion began to know and love the music. Her father had the score and often played small excerpts from the opera at home. Joan Cross then the Director of Sadlers Wells and who was to sing Ellen Orford at the premier would come to the house to practise with Peter Pears as Peter Grimes. Marion went to most of the rehearsals. On the day of the dress rehearsal, she was supposed to take an exam at the Royal College of Music, but she could not resist the temptation to watch the rehearsal. She skipped the exam. Clifford Curzon, her mentor and a stickler for practice did not forgive her for some time. But it was worth it. The opening night was a thrilling occasion, a new beginning for English opera. And Marion's recollection of the occasion was vivid:

"I remember wearing my first evening dress – lent to me by my former headmistress Miss Burke (who was a very elegant woman), as clothes rationing was of course still in force. Afterwards there was a party at the Savoy. When we finally got to bed, we were kept awake by the loud miaowing of amorous cats, who used to raid the dustbins of the 'Home and Colonial' grocer under our maisonette. Ben's bedroom was above mine, and I went out on to the adjacent balcony where the coal was kept, to throw coal at them. At the same time Ben had gone to the bathroom above to throw water at them – which of course landed on me! Hysterics all round – and we ended up having tea in the kitchen at dawn."[13]

Marion was by now a very attractive young woman. John Amis,[14] who described Marion's father as an absent-minded professor, never without spectacles on his nose, was surprised that he had fathered such an exceedingly beautiful girl. Ronald Duncan remembered Marion's good looks too. In 1945 he was busy writing the libretto of *The Rape of Lucretia* for Britten. The composer had chosen his new opera to star contralto Kathleen Ferrier in the title role although by that time he had not even started on the score. Although he was devoted to his glamorous wife Rose

Marie, who was at that time ill with tuberculosis, Duncan liked attractive women and had a roving eye. One morning he was working, as usual, in Britten and Pears' house in St John's Wood and was trying to decide how to describe Lucretia sleeping. He decided to take a break from his work and take an early cup of tea to Marion, whose bedroom was next to the kitchen. He tiptoed in, "unaware that I was enacting Tarquinius' stealthy walk through the sleeping house towards Lucretia's bed." Unlike Tarquinius he put the cup down and sat down to watch Marion as she slept on. He picked up a pencil and wrote down what he saw:

She sleeps as a rose
Upon the night
And light as lily
That floats on a lake…
There sleeps Lucretia…

Then he tiptoed out of the room and put the lullaby on Britten's desk.[15]

Perhaps missing the music exam for Britten's rehearsal was indicative of where Marion's priorities lay at that time. She did not think she was learning enough at the Royal College of Music and spent what she felt were two rather unsuccessful terms there, taking piano lessons with Kendall Taylor and theory with Herbert Howells. Still aware that her piano technique needed a lot of development but rather disillusioned with her progress, she left the College and began lessons with Franz Osborn, a Jewish refugee from Berlin, who she says "was an excellent teacher, loosening up my technique and getting me going."

Marion's adult social and professional life soon began in earnest: meetings with friends, piano lessons with Clifford Curzon, concerts and theatre dates all appear in her increasingly full diaries. She was interested in all the arts, and throughout her life was curious in what was new in the art world. She went twice to the Picasso Matisse exhibition at the Victoria and Albert Museum in January 1946. The exhibition was intended to be a cultural exchange between Britain and France after the war but attracted a storm of controversy. Unlike Marion, many other patrons from South Kensington were not ready for such work.

Marion's career as a pianist began, at first with small performances. She became a member of the Apollo Society, and worked for some years with the group of poets, actors and musicians whose purpose was to design and perform programmes of poetry and music. For each event, the Society put together a mix of performances chosen for the client organisation and then sent along those they thought right to deliver them. Marion was in very good company. The list of poets connected with the Society included T S Eliot, Walter de la Mare, Cecil Day Lewis and Edith Sitwell, to name just a few, and the very long list of readers contains famous actors of their generation. Peggy Ashcroft, Joyce Grenfell, Alec Guinness, Celia Johnson, Sybil Thorndike and many others who were re-invigorating their careers after the war. Marion found herself booked for events in London with the Apollo but also across the country. In the 1945-46 season, for example, she played Mozart's Sonata in F major for the Hill Music Club on December 12. Still with the Society she played at the Wulfrun Hall in Wolverhampton, October 5 1948, the Apollo group being booked by Wolverhampton's Civic Hall Arts Society. A programme of lunchtime concerts at the Fleur-de Lis Hall in Fetter Lane EC4 gave her plenty of work in the 1947-48 season. The admission to the just under an hour-long concert cost 1 shilling, (less than £2 today) and a buffet was provided from 12.30 to 2.15. Marion often played as a piano soloist and sometimes with a violinist friend Winifred Roberts, who later married Geraint Jones the organist. Winifred (Win) remained a staunch friend and ally until the end of her life. Marion also formed a piano duo with Catherine Shanks, a fellow pupil at the Royal College of Music. They played works – many by Mozart and Schubert – for four hands at one keyboard. She began to be known in the music business and her correspondence from the time shows the arrangements for many bookings, the programme, fees and travel arrangements. A photograph by David Gurney for Associated press in 1947, now in the National Portrait Gallery collection shows her beautiful and dressed elegantly in evening dress sitting at her piano.

Her close friendship with Benjamin Britten proved useful to her burgeoning career. In summer 1947 Ben's English Opera Group was performing his children's opera, *Let's Make an Opera* in Aldeburgh and then taking it on a tour including Cheltenham and Wolverhampton. Marion was booked as a pianist for 12 guineas a week for performing, and for attendance at the June rehearsals she was paid at 3 guineas per session. With Catherine she played the duet in Britten's cantata with music, *St Nicholas* on June 11 at the Aldeburgh Festival of 1949, fee 4 guineas. Perhaps prophetically, Marion was booked for a Rural Music Schools Association Festival Concert at

Southwark Cathedral, on June 23 that year. The president of the Association was George Lascelles, the young Earl Harewood.

Marion still lived at home with her parents, Britten and Pears, but in spring 1946, that home changed yet again. Benjamin Britten had flown out to the US after receiving an upsetting cable from Eric Crozier about how rehearsals for the first American production of *Peter Grimes* were proceeding at the summer school at Tanglewood, Massachusetts. It was chaotic he said, "Musicians were painting backdrops or operating the lighting plot when they should have been in rehearsals: singers spent time in madrigal groups instead of learning the opera's difficult choruses...."[16] Britten was very disappointed with the student performance, describing it to his American friends the Mayers, as a bad nightmare. After waiting for a much-delayed flight home, Britten returned to England somewhat jaundiced against America. During his absence, Peter Pears, with Erwin's help, had negotiated the lease on a large Victorian house at 3 Oxford Square in Paddington. Ben, Peter, Marion and the other Steins moved in. Pears had elderly parents, who he felt needed to be near him, and wanted them to live in the house too. In retrospect this was not a successful arrangement. It was a large household with Pears' parents on the ground floor, the Steins and Britten and Pears on the second, a room for the housekeeper Mrs Hurley, and one for Eric Crozier, the librettist, in the attic. Sophie took over the running of the household as she had done in St John's Wood. When in London, Britten and Pears ate their meals with the Steins.

Paul Kildea describes the situation in the house, "The

Steins came with the furniture, and Pears' elderly parents moved in as well, soon thereafter objecting to the food, to Sophie's running of the house and to Marion's piano playing."[17] Eric Crozier, who lived in the attic room recalled the same time in his autobiography.

"It was a district of huge early Victorian houses. In theory the plan was a good one. Peter had two elderly parents who needed somewhere to live so what could be better for them to make their home with him and Ben, plus of course, the Erwin Stein family, and for Sophie to manage the housekeeping.... a courageous and cheerful woman she was run off her feet trying to manage the house and conjure up three meals a day from the antediluvian kitchen in the basement. Mr and Mrs Pears, a stiff necked and rather arrogant couple, did not like the Steins. They objected to the food, criticised Sophie, and they went out of their way in general to make mischief. They strongly objected too, to Marion's piano playing. She was now eighteen or nineteen, a pretty girl who had recently begun studying the piano in earnest, and she had a basement room where she used sometime to practice four or five hours a day. The elderly Pears hated it .... So did the old man who lived in the enormous house next door ... He used to hammer violently on the party wall."[18]

Over forty years later, in 1990, Marion too recounted her own memories of that time in the Pears Britten house. She recalled that the mixed household was not always easy. Mrs Pears could be jealous of Marion's mother who ran the house, particularly when Pears paid more attention to Sophie. "There was a curmudgeonly old neighbour, who objected to noise coming from our house, and would wave a stick at me from the pavement above. He couldn't do much about the sound coming from the big L-shaped drawing room on the first floor, where we would on many occasions play piano duets, Ben, Peter, my father and I, in various combinations."[19]

In October 1947, Mrs Pears died and Mr Pears a few months later. The house was now too big for the Britten/Pears extended family. In autumn 1948, when Marion was studying for a short time in Belgium, her parents moved to their own home, 22 Melbury Road, London W14, just off Kensington High Street. Aunt Laura lived in the same road. Now the housing situation was reversed. Britten and Pears rented two rooms from the Steins for when they were in London, and Sophie was always delighted when 'the boys' were back. But increasingly, Ben and Peter concentrated on their life in Aldeburgh.

Until the move to Melbury Road Marion had spent important teenage years living in a house with Britten and Pears. In later years there was some speculation as to Marion's knowledge of, and attitude to, homosexuality. But Marion was never naïve. She must have been well aware of the relationship between Benjamin and Peter, a relationship accepted by all their friends and musical acquaintances, despite homosexual acts still being illegal until 1967. Marion lived in close proximity with them in the house, and would know they shared a bedroom and a bed. Although she never openly said she approved of homosexuality and some years later decried it at least once when challenged, she must have been comfortable and non-judgemental with gay friends from an early age; something that stood her in good stead in her future life.

Her close friendship with Britten lasted for many years until his death and during that time she stayed with Ben and Pears at their homes in Suffolk regularly and often travelled with the couple. Ben made friends easily but shed them very quickly if anything happened that upset him or he felt they were taking advantage of him. Marion was one of the very few friends whose friendship he valued all his life.

Now regularly performing as a piano duo, Marion and Catherine attracted admirers. Marion was tall, dark and slim and considered a beauty, but at 21, there was no young man who tempted her sufficiently to give up her burgeoning career. In the summer of 1947 Benjamin Britten, in a letter to her father Erwin, said he was "glad that Marion enjoyed her performing – that's half the battle."[20]

Marion seemed to be settled into a life as a performer, at least for the foreseeable future.

But the following year, her life took a most unexpected course.

In the June of 1948, Marion went to her friend Benjamin Britten's first Aldeburgh Festival. Although living in London for most of the time, the composer had started to base himself in Suffolk, using a legacy from his mother to buy The Old Mill at Snape. In 1947 he bought the larger Crag House, overlooking the sea at 4 Crabbe Street Aldeburgh. The sea, visible from his house, was a continuing source of inspiration for his music. His love for Suffolk and his Aldeburgh Festival, begun in 1948, saw him putting down his roots in the town for the rest of his life. His first festival. a celebration of music, was the first of many, occasions which are now a key feature of the musical year in the UK. Britten's *Albert Herring*, premiered a year before at Glyndebourne, was the featured opera, with Peter Pears and Joan Cross singing the main roles. A host of other performances, piano, song and poetry recitals, chamber music and other concerts took place at many locations in and around the Aldeburgh area. As well as using the Jubilee Hall, just along the street from Britten's house, other local venues were pressed into use including the Aldeburgh Parish Church, as well as nearby Orford Church, Framlingham Church and Blythburgh Church. The sleepy Aldeburgh area was suddenly full of music lovers. Marion of course, was there to celebrate the new festival with her friends Ben and Peter. She loved Ben's music and she would not miss the event for anything.

Among the most enthusiastic other lovers of music there, and particularly of opera, was a young man up from Cambridge University. The handsome 25-year-old George Lascelles, the King's nephew, and cousin to the future Queen Elizabeth II, had recently inherited the title of 7th Earl of Harewood and the house that went with it, the beautiful 18th century Harewood House in West Yorkshire. Lascelles had an exciting recent past. He had spent the war as a captain in the Grenadier Guards, been wounded and taken prisoner at Monte Como on 18 June 1944 and imprisoned at Colditz. He and other *Prominente,* prisoners, those with any sort of illustrious connection, were kept there as hostages, probably with a possibility of being use as bargaining chips if needed. As the end of the war became inevitable, they were moved frequently across Germany by their captors, ahead of the fast-approaching allies. Eventually they arrived at Stalag XVIII C prisoner of war camp at Markt Pongau in what had been Austria. Hitler had signed George's death warrant in March 1945 and in the camp, Obergruppenfuhrer Gottlaob Berger told the prisoners that he had received orders to shoot them. However, realising that the war was within a couple of days of its end, and that he might need something to argue in mitigation of his role in the conflict, he said that he was going to disobey the orders. It was pointless to keep the group as prisoners. He was going to hand them over to the Swiss who would conduct them through German lines and into Allied hands, and this he did. Eventually George arrived back in England and spent the summer at Harewood recuperating from his ordeal. Demobilized in December 1946, he spent a short time as aide-de-camp to Canada's governor-general before going up to King's College, Cambridge to continue his delayed education. He read English there, getting to know E. M. (Morgan) Forster, already friendly with Benjamin Britten, whose *The Rape of Lucretia* Lascelles had recently heard at Glyndebourne. From his early childhood, through his teenage years and even in Colditz where he listened to records and claimed to have learned a lot, he developed his interest in music. By the time he left Cambridge his tastes had evolved particularly toward opera and by 1948 he was a keen devotee. His ambition was to work in an opera house.

He was, it is said, the first Englishman to be smitten by the singing of Maria Callas, hearing her sing in La Gioconda in Verona in August 1947. Hearing her again in 1951, and by then the editor of the magazine Opera, newly split from Ballet and Opera, he was entranced by her singing and her personality. He was delighted when David

Webster, the Chief Administrator of Covent Garden, and his new boss, secured her to sing Norma in 1952.

His relationship with Benjamin Britten began in 1947 too. Lascelles had met the composer only a few times, but encouraged by Morgan Forster he accepted Britten's invitation, although with a few personal misgivings about his youth, to become president of the newly-founded Aldeburgh Festival. He took to his role enthusiastically, bringing down a group of his Cambridge friends by bus to see Britten's opera *Albert Herring* at the Jubilee Hall.

It was at this first festival, from the 5-8 June 1948 that the attractive and lively twenty-one-year-old Marion first met the country's most eligible bachelor, the attractive and dashing George Lascelles, the new Earl of Harewood. The introduction of his friend Marion to the Earl must have been just one of many such introductions made by Britten to his new President, and possibly brief. In his autobiography George says that his first meeting with Marion was probably at that first Aldeburgh Festival and that she was at Cambridge for the 1948 May balls. But maybe because of the many people he was introduced to by Britten, and the fact that both he and Marion were likely to have been with other partners at the Cambridge balls, she did not make an immediate impression on him.

Getting to know her had to wait until later that summer.[21]

TWO

FOUR

George

arion began to enjoy herself after the initial period of post-war gloom. In the summer of 1948, she went on holiday to Austria with a cousin, her first significant trip abroad since the end of the war. She must have written excitedly about it to her friend Benjamin Britten as in a letter to her father Erwin, Britten commented, "I gather Marion's having a time and a half." George Lascelles too was in Austria that summer. For him also, life was opening up after the war and with two friends he drove to their first post-war foreign festival at Salzburg. In George's case, the trip was to hear the Mozart operas, particularly *Fidelio*. Although it was an hour away from Salzburg, the threesome chose to stay at the famous White Horse Inn, the Weisses Rossi. On their last evening in the hotel, he noticed that there was a new arrival from England, "A very pretty girl.... Just arrived with a Viennese cousin.[22] It was Marin Stein, the girl he had met briefly at the Aldeburgh Festival earlier in the summer.

After that second brief encounter, they did not meet

again until the end of the year when Marion came back from a short study trip to Belgium. The attractive young woman had made an impression on George in Austria the previous summer, and he still remembered her. He contacted Marion and took her out a few times just after Christmas. Their relationship was conducted mostly through attending concerts, opera going, and dinners. When George drove Marion back to Melbury Gardens after a night out, another courting couple, Moira Shearer, a star of the Royal Ballet, and journalist Ludovic Kennedy, would often be across the road saying goodnight.

Marion's family and friends were obviously curious about the growing interest that Marion and George Lascelles had in each other. Benjamin Britten, writing to Peter Pears 4 January 1949, refers to a party which Lascelles attended, saying that he "expected Sophie was in a state of nice excitement because Lascelles was there."[23] In March 1949 the BBC broadcast a concert performance of Alban Berg's *Wozzeck* and Marion accompanied George to rehearsals and the performance. Things got serious, Marion said, after this performance of Wozzeck. Her father remarked that this dark story of death and destruction with its prominent themes of militarism, callousness and sadism was not exactly the story to start a romance. But whatever he thought about the opera, George was now convinced that this was the girl he wanted to marry. He went up to Harewood and, on a walk in the grounds, told his mother, the Princess Royal, of his intentions.

It was not going to be an easy courtship. The reaction of his mother was "Good God" and then an initial silence. After then asking a series of questions about Marion, including could she cook, she said that she wanted to see her. The potential bride was invited to stay at Harewood. What Marion felt when she saw the magnificent 18th century Harewood House, set in a landscape of 1,000 acres designed by Lancelot (Capability) Brown, I can only guess. The change from a small house in London to these palatial surroundings must have been unimaginable. Being 'looked over' by George's mother cannot have been easy either. Princess Mary would not be an immediately comfortable mother-in-law. She supposedly said of her proposed daughter in law that 'not only is she Jewish.... she doesn't hunt;' for Princess Mary, two important failings. However, the visit went well. Although Marion said that Princess Mary was even more shy than she was, they went for a walk in the grounds. The lady-in-waiting, Phyllis Balfour, diplomatically took George aside so that the Princess and Marion could talk. After a short, embarrassed silence, Marion was asked "Can you cook?" Why this was a question and why it mattered to the Princess seems odd, as the family employed cooks. But perhaps it was the first thing she thought of. Marion had rarely cooked as Sophie looked after meals in the Stein household but she must have said something to suggest she could. According to the family, Marion was always known in the family as a terrible cook and never mastered the art. At the end of the visit, George's mother offered to write to the King on his behalf asking permission for her son to marry.

The complications of such a proposed marriage were many. George Lascelles was the son of The Princess Royal, the King's sister, and was then 11th in line to the throne. As such, the Earl had to seek permission from the King to marry. George went to see the King who seemed to be quite happy with the arrangement and thought it natural that he wanted to marry someone with similar musical tastes even though he, the King, had no such interests. However, the King was not prepared to give his consent until Queen Mary, his mother, had agreed. This was much more problematical as, although George did not know it at the time, Queen Mary had "already expressed herself as vigorously opposed to the whole idea." She was "In a great state and won't talk about it."[24]It is unlikely that George told Marion about such opposition, it would have been very hurtful. He waited a little time and then went to see his grandmother with whom he had always got on well. Eventually she made no more objections and Marion was taken to call on her. She was given the gift of a star sapphire pendant which later she wore as a ring. The next hurdle was an inspection by the Queen, Elizabeth, King George VI's wife. It was arranged that this would take place at Tommy Lascelle's house at St James's Palace. Sir Alan Lascelles (Tommy) was a first cousin of George's father and secretary to the King. Tommy's daughter was engaged to be married and the wedding presents were being displayed at her home. "Quite by chance," recalled Marion, "the Queen was to come to tea and view the presents, and I would happen to be there! I must have passed muster, because shortly after that George went to see his uncle (the King), and my parents were invited to a Buckingham Palace Garden party and were presented to the King and Queen."[25] On 19 July 1949, the engagement was announced.

Although it was George's mother and grandma who had initial doubts about the suitability of the marriage rather than the Earl, Marion herself had some qualms about her future life as a Countess and as the chatelaine of the huge and beautiful Harewood House. Life in a middle-class London suburb had not prepared her for such. She wrote to her good friend Benjamin Britten asking for his advice on her relationship with Harewood. Relatively new to English Society, she wanted to know if a commoner could hope to sustain such a relationship in such a society. On the 7 April 1949, he replied. His nice letter recommended that she go ahead if she loved George, that the difficulties owing to his position may not arise, and if they did, she had good friends who would stand by her "through thick and thin"

"Forgive the avuncular advice."[26]

She did love George, as he did her. But it must have been comforting to know that her friends would support her, whatever happened in the future.

There was to be no more privacy. From relative obscurity up to that point, Marion would suddenly become a much-photographed and written-about member of the aristocracy. Cecil Beaton, the society photographer of the time took her picture. In the week after the engagement, Pathé newsreel cameras caught her for the first time outside her house. looking chic in full-skirted dress with a wide white collar, bolero jacket and small flowered hat as, trying to avoid the photographers, she took a taxi from her home in Kensington to Buckingham Palace. Movietone's coverage of the engagement, with the title 'Lord Harewood's Romance' and spread across the newsreel screen, showed the couple at the Buckingham Palace Garden party on 25 July 1949. According to the voice-over, "everyone was looking for them" and the camera caught them first talking to the Duke of Edinburgh and later walking into the palace from the garden.[27] That summer must have been a very busy time for George and Marion. On the 26 July, 23-year-old Princess Elizabeth and her husband Prince Philip arrived by train in York for a visit to Yorkshire. Based at Harewood, the couple were accompanied on many of their visits round the county by Princess Mary and George.

Marion had her own busy life that summer, preparing for a major change in her life. As soon as the wedding was announced Marion somehow became public property. The idea of a girl from an ordinary middle-class home, and a refugee too, marrying into the royal family, captured the public imagination, especially that of women. There were hundreds of letters from friends but most from people who did not know her. They came from all over the country but also from Australia, Canada, Hong Kong, South Africa and beyond. They were from individuals, 'Maria from Yorkshire', and from groups, 'the Staff of West London Sorting Office'. There were many gifts accompanying letters of congratulation, all of which were acknowledged by the secretary and signed by Marion. A powder compact, a piece of Spanish Lace, a scrap book of press cuttings about Marion and George, a tie clip, small pieces of silver, a picture of edelweiss, and poems were just some of the presents, sometimes accompanied by claimed links to the couple: a shared anniversary, similar musical interests, a memory of a concert. The widow of Richard Tauber, who had remarried, sent an autograph of Gustav Mahler, but also suggested that Marion and George might like to use her husband's art studio for their theatre décor. There was the rather precipitate offer of a christening robe by the 75-year-old widow of an Austrian professor.

Some of the letters, while congratulatory, also included requests for favours. Writers of songs and small pieces of music sent them with requests for them to be played or Marion's influence used to recommend them. People asked for contributions to magazines, for photographs, for autographs. And some of the favours requested were for presents. One woman in South Africa asked for a suit that she had seen Marion wear in a photograph, to be sent out to her. "she was the same size", and another asked Marion to buy a piano for her granddaughter. And a Mrs Johnson in Portsmouth asked Marion to have the Princess Royal send her a small piece of the wedding cake!

But there were sad letters too. These must have been upsetting. Marion was suddenly cast in the role of benefactor and while her husband did later have a fund to help people in need, it was strange to think that Marion's correspondents would think that this young bride suddenly had a bottomless fund of money to distribute. Refugees from Hitler who had not been so lucky as she in their new lives sent her letters in German. One British mother of fourteen sent a harrowing tale of misery with a request for money. An old orchestral bass player who was disabled and could not transport his bass any distance asked for booking contacts near to his home, a grandmother asked for help for her granddaughter who had injured her arm.

However, a charming letter from Adelina de Lara in Woking must have been welcome. It was one of congratulations from the last surviving pupil of Clara Schumann. "As the oldest of all women pianists I allow myself the privilege and honour of writing to you to express my congratulations."

One letter that was sent to Erwin and Sophie, probably by Erwin's eccentric older sister Paula, was unlikely to have been shown to Marion. As she did often, Paula. from her home in Ceylon (Sri Lanka), sent personal horoscopes that she had cast for them to family members. This letter contained carefully drawn and analysed horoscopes of both Marion and George, purporting to predict their life together. Whilst most of the analysis pointed to their lives in music and art, Paula did write that Marion's horoscope predicted major problems in life which would have to be overcome. The letter and diagrams stayed firmly in the older couple's correspondence file, never to be disclosed to the new bride.

Not only the public considered Marion now 'theirs' but the Press too went to town. From this point onwards, Marion would have to get used to the intrusion of the press and work hard to protect her privacy. She was described by some as aloof. Those who knew her say she could do regal when she wanted but this front was protective. As a private person she was lively, funny, and friendly. She had to develop both a private and public persona, as do many in the public eye. She had to learn to ignore things written or said about her that were wrong, half-true or even hurtful. At the time of her engagement and wedding there were articles in magazines and newspapers, many sentimental about the 'Cinderella' story and of variable accuracy. One schmalzy article in a woman's magazine kept in Marion's archive begins:

"There she goes, bless her, she's just like Cinderella!" cried a stout, motherly-looking woman, her voice sounding clearly for a moment above the cheers." It goes on to describe the meeting of the couple by the sea in Aldeburgh, totally imaginary journalism.

"Naturally enough, Benjamin introduces his two friends one night after the music. Marion has heard a lot about George, whose name and writings are always being talked about in musical circles; George too, has been told about Marion's piano playing, but they have never met. Right away, the two find much in common; they walk together talking music while the soft summer breeze blows in from the sea. Unheard by them, music is borne on the breeze, the first strains of a love motif."

Later in the article, describing a scene at the wedding, the same journalist comments on Marion's background.

"Interest ran high, for George Henry Hubert Lascelles, seventh Earl of Harewood, was, at twenty-six, the most eligible bachelor in the country, and scores of society girls in the crowded pews waited with envy in their hearts for a glimpse of the Viennese beauty who had carried off the season's most coveted matrimonial prize. Marion, to most of them, was as much a stranger as she was to the girls outside. Of foreign birth, from a comparatively obscure home, she had never been presented at Court, had even worked for her living, and here she was, central figure in the most fashionable wedding of the year."

My goodness! She had 'even worked for a living.'

No wonder Marion said she was so bored of all the tasteless press cuttings that she was sent.

Whether she liked it or not, the Press would become part of Marion's life in many ways. They would support her, praise her, comment on her looks, and record her life as a public figure. In October, just before the wedding, her father wrote to her, "We see pictures of you almost daily in the papers and you both look cheerful as is fitting. It appears that your wedding has made a multitude of people – in some misterious (sic) way – happy, although they had nothing whatsoever to do with it."

In later years the press would prove an intrusion and something she had to fight, but in 1949 they loved her. She was 'Cinderella' and her handsome prince had arrived.

FIVE

The Wedding of the Year

The date was set for 10 November 1949.

To organise such a grand and lavish Royal wedding, in the comparatively short time between the engagement of George and Marion in July and the ceremony in November needed a lot of organisation. The couple needed to sort out the venues, the guest list and the honeymoon; Benjamin Britten and Ronald Duncan started to write a wedding anthem. George's younger brother Gerald, was called back from inspecting his sugar properties in Barbados to take charge of all the minutiae of wedding preparation. According to George, Gerald was assigned everything beginning with 'P', "ranging from Parking of cars to Presents for the bridesmaids."[28] Reminiscing about that time, George recalled that the organisation of the wedding anthem which was proving difficult for the church choir to perform, was allocated to Gerald, by assuring him that the anthem was often called Partitura. Despite the rush, everything was done on time.

The wedding was, Carol Kennedy states, "as in the

old days, an occasion of almost feudal celebration."[29] Two hundred of Harewood's farm, estate and household workers were taken by a special train to London for the ceremony. Cliff Lancaster, who worked on the estate for 27 years recalled "We filled a whole train. The Princess paid for the train there and back, we just had to pay for our lunch. We got taken to St James's Palace for a buffet do and we were shown into a room with photos of King George. We came back on the 11.30 train from King's Cross."[30]

It was unseasonably warm and dry that November Thursday and occasional sunlight broke through the clouds. Crowds, in light coats and cardigans packed the area outside St Mark's Church, North Audley Street in Mayfair, hoping to get a glimpse of the couple and all the royals who were to attend. This opportunity for ordinary people to see a royal wedding with all the richness and style associated with it, must have been a great draw. As had been her mother-in-law, the Princess Mary's wedding 27 years before, Marion's too was a grand occasion and very welcome in the aftermath of a world war. The four years since the end of WW2 had been those of increasing austerity, and rationing on many goods, especially food, was still making life difficult for many. Clothes rationing, which had meant increasing drabness on the streets despite people's attempts to make-do and mend, only ended in May 1949. There was a significant difference between the appearance of the onlookers and the glamour of the arriving guests. Movie cameras captured the excitement of the crowd as the smiling King George V1 and his Queen, a fur coat round her shoulders, accompanied by the rather glum looking eighteen-year-old Princess Margaret, arrived at the church. Such was the importance of this wedding that the royal family had made a special journey from Balmoral and would return there after the reception. The crowds were not disappointed as other important guests, Princess Elizabeth and Prince Philip, the Earl's mother the Princess Royal, the bride's mother in a dress and hat of parma violet, and Lady Churchill arrived along with many of the titled aristocracy. Princess Marina, Duchess of Kent, the widow of George's uncle and his namesake, was the only royal conspicuously absent although her three children attended. According to the Jewish press, her excuse of having to go abroad was unconvincing. [31]

Most of the guests were already in the church, waiting for the ceremony to begin. The world of music, so important to both the bride and groom, was well represented. Benjamin Britten, known for usually avoiding weddings, and his partner Peter Pears, were already preparing to perform the anthem that Britten had written to celebrate the occasion. Susanna Walton, the wife of the composer William Walton recalled later that when Britten and Pears appeared dressed as choirboys in white surplices over red cassocks, she and her husband burst into giggles. They had to be shushed by their neighbours in the next pew, artist John Piper and his librettist wife Myfanwy.[32] The ten minute *A Wedding Anthem (Amo Ergo Sum) op.46*, words by Ronald Duncan, soloists Peter Pears and Joan Cross, was too much for King George V1. Contemporary music was not King George's metier and according to the observant Duncan, the King sat through the whole ten minutes looking very bored.[33]

Whilst Britten and Pears were preparing to perform the anthem, the bride was driving the four miles to the church with her father Erwin. The newsreel cameras captured the scene as she left her parents modest Kensington house and arrived in Mayfair. Marion looked wonderful. Her bridal outfit was a timeless style which any bride today could wear. The silver and white dress, a gift from Princess Mary, was fitted to show off her slender figure. The material was French brocade, and Marion wore the Princess Royal's train and veil, held in place on her dark hair by a floral headdress. Two of Marion's close friends were adult bridesmaids. One was her piano-playing partner the 24-year-old Catherine Shanks, the other was Lydia Brennan a schoolfriend, who had only left school that year. The younger members of the wedding party were from George's circle. Sarah Lanyon, a very excited eight-year-old bridesmaid was the daughter of a family friend, Norman Lanyon. Davina Lloyd, only six, was the daughter of the Second Baron Lloyd, one of the Lascelles family. The older bridesmaids wore off the shoulder, fitted dresses and white glove and wore floral wreaths on their heads. They carried sheaves of flowers. The smaller ones had white full skirted frocks with puffed sleeves, flowers in their hair and carried posies. Completing the party was the three-year-old Hon Malcolm Forbes, (later the 23rd Lord Forbes of Forbes Castle Aberdeenshire), in a white frilled shirt. The wedding photographs show his dark hair neatly slicked down and a determined look on his face. Being the page at a royal wedding was obviously a great responsibility for him, and he took it seriously.

After the forty-five-minute service, the bride and groom emerged to a rapturous welcome from the crowd who tried hard to get a good view of the couple. George went against wedding etiquette by getting into the bridal car first leaving Marion to climb in after him with her full dress and train. He remembered it as a decision he made thinking it would be easier for Marion. It seems unlikely that anyone held it against him. The good-natured smiling police, helmets firmly in place, formed a cordon by linking arms as people surged forward to get a glimpse of the couple, many holding up mirrors, (there were no mobile phones then) to get a view. More people lined the route to St James's Palace where the reception was held, and the crowd was rewarded in their wait to see the arrival of 82-year-old Queen Mary, the widow of George V, who did not attend the wedding but went to the reception. The short-sighted Morgan Forster told the story of how, at St James's, he saw a tall white figure standing by the window. Thinking it was Queen Mary, he approached to pay his respects – to find it was in fact the wedding cake! Some hours later, Marion and George emerged from St James's Palace in a shower of rose petals to set out for their honeymoon in Paris. Their car was decorated with symbols of good luck for newlyweds, white heather tied on to the bonnet and a white high-heeled shoe tied on behind.

A long honeymoon followed all the excitement of the wedding. In Paris the newly-married couple were given Marlene Dietrich's bed which was much too short for George and his feet hung out over the end. But as he commented in his autobiography, "to complain about the bed on one's honeymoon did not seem quite the thing." They went sightseeing in Paris, managing to shake off what they thought was a persistent journalist, only to find he was a French detective, assigned to them for security.

From Paris it was on to Venice where they stayed in the same hotel that George's parents had chosen for their own honeymoon in 1922 and Rome and Naples were followed by twelve days in a villa on Capri. There the couple met Cecil Gray the composer and writer. Marion warned George that his reputation as a drinker was considerable but he was very good company, kind and amusing which was, as George commented, at odds with his 'vinegar pen'. Gray introduced the couple to the writer Norman Douglas, who had broken bail conditions when on trial for pederasty in 1917, fled the country and exiled himself, eventually to Capri. Invited to lunch with Douglas, now an old man, Marion and George listened as he talked captivatingly about Capri and music.

And then it was the ferry to Naples and the flight home.

A new life was beginning for Marion, now Countess of Harewood.

SIX

Countess

Although Harewood House in Yorkshire was George's ancestral home and the couple would spend much time there, Marion and George wanted a London base. For a short while after their marriage, and while they searched for a house, the couple lived in rooms that had been George's father's London home at St James's Palace on Pall Mall. It was not easy to find the house they wanted in a London which was still recovering from wartime bombing. Friends tried to help with suggestions; Maurice McMillan, a politician and the son of the future prime minister, was selling his house in Gloucester Crescent they were told. There was a house near Park Lane which was war-damaged, but licenced for conversion. They despaired of finding a suitable home in London. But at last, Two Orme Square, then owned by the chairman of Barclay's bank came available. An austere very late Georgian house at the top of the Square, just off the Bayswater Road, it was once home to Lord Leighton the famous painter. In the front garden, just by the gates on to the Bayswater Road, stands the sculpture of an eagle on a tall plinth. Probably a Russian eagle, although with only one head (a Russian eagle has two), it is thought to have been erected by the developer of Orme square, Edward Orme, in the early 1820s to celebrate links with Russia. Tsar Alexander I of Russia had visited London in 1814 and Orme's Moscow Road and St Petersburgh Place developments were started in 1815. Whether the eagle commemorates this visit, the victory at Waterloo or an astute business deal involving the sale of local gravel to Russia, is still debated.[34]

The house suited Marion and George. It had a big drawing room, as well as a sitting room and dining room on the ground floor. There were ample bedrooms, a kitchen and a small cottage over the garage, thought to have been where Leighton's models dressed. There was plenty of space for a piano. Entertaining in London would be easy in such a house. But of course, the huge and beautiful Harewood Hall, in Yorkshire, quite large enough to accommodate the Earl and his new wife and any potential family as well as his mother, was home too, and the young Earl and Countess took up residence. Eventually George's aunt persuaded Princess Mary to relinquish her downstairs rooms to the young couple and move upstairs to a large bedroom. with a dressing room and bathroom. She kept her lovely south-facing sitting room downstairs sitting room, a room which had been designed for her when she and her husband had first moved to Harewood. Marion converted the Princess's dressing room into her own sitting room, to hold a desk and, of course, a piano.

The new owners were thus established. But how would

it work to have two women sharing the role of chatelaine to one of the finest houses in the country?

It would not be easy. Marion and her mother-in-law were very different people. Victoria Alexandra Alice Mary, always known as Princess Mary, was, as Elizabeth Basford writes in her insightful biography,[35] a very modern princess, well before Princess Diana was given that epithet. As a young girl she had visited factories, hospitals and children's homes with her mother and took on a natural caring role as the only girl in a family of six siblings. She was very close to her brother David, who was briefly King Edward VIII before his abdication, and she was also the sister of King George VI. As a young girl she longed to be a nurse and at eighteen she sought permission from her parents, the King and Queen, to train professionally, a rare request for a royal princess. Permission gained, she enrolled at Great Ormond Street Children's Hospital and worked in paediatrics. Many causes were close to her heart. One of her best-known initiatives was The Princess Mary Christmas gift boxes. In 1914 she set up a fund to send a present to 'everyone wearing the King's uniform on Christmas Day'. Each tin was decorated with an image of Mary and other military and imperial symbols and typically filled with an ounce of tobacco, a packet of cigarettes in a yellow monogrammed wrapper, a cigarette lighter, and a Christmas card and photograph from Princess Mary. Some contained sweets, chocolates, and lemon drops. It was a huge undertaking. Around 400,000 were delivered by that Christmas although it was 1920 before all service personnel had received one. In 1918, when she was only twenty-one, her father appointed Mary as Colonel in Chief of the Royal Scots, the oldest and most senior regiment in the British Army at the time, and she was known for taking a real interest in the men and their families. In 1918 too, she became the first member of the royal family to visit France following the Armistice. She visited centres associated with Queen Alexandra's Royal Army Nursing Corps.

By the end of the 1914-1918 war, Princess Mary was of marriageable age. However, due to the turbulence in Europe, the number of potential and suitable royal matches had dwindled. King George V and Queen Mary accepted that their children would look to members of the English and Scottish nobility rather than European royalty for their future spouses. Princess Mary had probably met Henry Lascelles, Viscount Harewood, still unmarried in his thirties, at house parties at Chatsworth and Bolton Abbey and he had also been a house guest at Balmoral, Windsor and Sandringham. It was a love match, certainly for the Princess, right from the start. Princess Mary, so members of her household believed, formed such an attachment to the tall, fair-moustached Henry Lascelles that "had she not been able to have him, she would have remained unmarried", as one member of that household recalled sixty years later.[36] In November 1921, Lascelles proposed to the twenty-four-year-old Mary and was willingly accepted. Both families were delighted. Four months later, Henry George Charles Lascelles, Viscount Harewood, married Princess Mary in Westminster Abbey on an unseasonably warm winter's day, Tuesday 28 February 1922. It was a welcome opportunity for the country to rejoice at the royal wedding of 'our beloved princess', and to enjoy royal pageantry once again, as the country emerged from post-war weariness.

After the wedding the Queen gave a party for guests which included tenants from the King's and Harewood's estates, a way of rewarding tenants and household staff, replicated at Marion's wedding over a quarter of a century later. After a honeymoon in Shropshire and Italy, the young couple returned to take up residence at Goldsborough, near Knaresborough in Yorkshire. a Jacobean mansion owned by the Lascelles family.

After her marriage and then becoming a mother in 1923, she did not confine her interests solely to the family. Becoming a Countess and moving into Harewood House in 1929 when her husband inherited the title, she continued to expand her patronages in her northern home, among them her support of the Leeds Triennial Music Festival, the Yorkshire Ladies Council of Leeds Education and Leeds Infirmary. Mary, although a shy young woman, continued as a countess to be highly involved in national organisations too. Between the wars she patronised many charities, particularly those connected with her interests in nursing, the women's services and the Girl Guides. In 1937, as President of the Girl Guides, she enrolled the princesses Elizabeth and Margaret into the first Buckingham Palace Brownie Pack and Guide Company. Seven-year-old Margaret became a brownie and was enrolled into the Leprechaun Six. The older Elizabeth became a second in the Kingfisher Patrol of the guides.

But in 1949, when her son brough home his new bride to Harewood, this very busy and talented woman was going through a difficult time. She had lost her husband Harry in May 1947 after celebrating twenty-five years of marriage earlier that year. It had been hoped that a visit to the Imperial hotel in Torquay for their anniversary would help to restore her husband's health which seemed to be in decline after several operations, no doubt worsened by anxiety in wartime about his son and heir who had been held captive in Germany. Despite such hopes for recovery, the sixth Earl Harewood died of a heart attack on the 24 May that year. His wife's cross of rhododendrons for her husband's funeral carried the note "In gratitude for twenty-five years of perfect love and companionship."[37] Mary missed him dreadfully. But stoically she continued to fulfil what she saw as her local and royal duties. On 21 July 1947, only two months after Harry died, she travelled to Lichfield in the Midlands to lay the foundation stone of a new cottage to be built on an historic site adjacent to St Chad's Well. The local newspaper of the time reported that wearing 'black mourning dress fronted with white lace, and a necklace of pearls', she attended a service in the cathedral and a garden party in the grounds of the Bishop's palace.

As well as the sadness of widowhood which she had to hide in public, she was faced with the sale of a large part of the estate and possessions due to a seventy percent death tax. For three years the new Earl and his mother had to negotiate what could be sold and what retained to make sure that the family could continue to live at Harewood. In his autobiography, George recalled, "In the end, sales took place three years after my father's death and we got rid of some two-thirds of the land and chattels. We gave a lunch for the tenants in a marquee in front of the house before announcing the sales. I had in a speech to admit that there was an element of farewell about the party, and shall never forget the collective intake of breath when I mentioned the death duty rate." [38] During these years too, the family had to spend a great deal of time putting the house back to normal, after it had been used as a wartime hospital since 1940. The hospital moved out of Harewood only a few weeks before Harry died and everything had to be unpacked and restored to its pre-war position or a new place found for it. There were also, as for many large estates in the country just post-war, difficult decisions to be made about its future. It cannot have been easy for Princess Mary to accept that if the house was going to survive financially, part of it would have to be opened to the public. From 1950, onwards, starting with just five of the state apartments, increasingly more parts of the house were open for public viewing. The house became an immediate attraction and in the late 1950s, the Harewoods moved upstairs to a new suite of rooms created from bedrooms on the first floor overlooking the north front. There was so much change that was hard for the Princess Royal. George and his brother Gerald noticed that their mother found it hard to cope after the death of her husband in 1947. She hated to be left alone for long and needed the support of family and close friends, especially those of her own age, around her.

Although she was known as a 'modern' princess by earlier standards, and still had a range of interests, she lived in a way that was not essentially different from that lived in the house before the war. She loved Harewood and it was her home. George described his mother as gentle and kind, "with in later life a little Hanoverian spleen underneath." She was "conditioned to communicate only on an uncontroversial a level as possible." Princess Mary was brought up to discourage "direct discussion or any display of emotion."[39]

Barely fifty years old when her husband died, she was not ready to retire into a dowager role. It was unlikely therefore, that given her situation in 1949 and her restrained character she would welcome any incoming daughter-in-law, whatever her background, with open arms.

She and Marion were very unlike in their interests. Princess Mary was a countrywoman at heart. She and her husband rode frequently and kept horses. They had similar interests in art, antiques and gardening. After Harry died, the Princess continued to play a full part in the estate, and was especially keen on her Red Poll cattle herd. She maintained an interest in a stud farm and attended horse racing events and was almost obsessive in maintaining aspects of the garden that her husband had loved. Lord Harewood recollected in his autobiography that Marion had no experience of living in a big house in the country and that her mother-in-law, who ordered food but assumed others cooked and did household chores, was no role model for a post-war bride. Princess Mary assumed that it was normal to have a lady-in-waiting, an anachronism in the 1950s. However, the new Earl and his Countess did establish themselves at Harewood, settling in to the rooms that had been prepared for them and they started to take on the responsibilities of the house and estate.

Although he never says openly in his autobiography, George was obviously aware of some tensions between the two women who were both chatelaines of Harewood. Marion never felt that she belonged at Harewood whilst to her husband it was his main home. He knew that Marion felt that Harewood was his mother's house more even than his. She never actually said this to her husband, was happy to spend time at Harewood, and George's mother was kind to her and supportive in many ways. But real home, for Marion, was in London, in Orme Square. This was in total contrast to her husband who regarded Harewood as his refuge and felt fully comfortable there. Although he had been brought up in the grand pre-war style, he had also known Harewood in wartime simplicity and was quite prepared to adapt to "any pattern which would maintain Harewood as my home."[40] Perhaps, as George surmised, Marion was a city girl. But given the slightly uneasy relationship with her mother-in law, maybe she preferred Orme Square because it was her own choice of a home, not just because it was in London. Had she been the only chatelaine of Harewood she may eventually have become interested in country pursuits, who knows? As it was, she supported her husband most enthusiastically in his musical interests, interests which she shared.

Her own professional life in music ended effectively overnight. "I got so far and let it go. I don't regret it", she said later. Marion had a new role as Countess of Harewood and she took to the life well. There was much entertaining at Harewood, as there had been in pre-war days. George's mother still dressed for dinner and when there were guests, the men wore dinner jackets. Leeds Festivals and the York Races saw many visitors and there were many others too who came on business related to the public services supported by George's mother. Family such as Erwin and Sophie, and personal friends, particularly

Benjamin Britten and his partner Peter Pears came up to Yorkshire frequently. Marion and George were great friends and fans of Britten and in March 1950 Marion used her Harewood name and developing organisational skills to create an opera-inspired fancy dress ball on behalf of Britten's fairly-new opera company, the English Opera Group. The cabaret included Frederick Ashton and Moira Shearer dancing the tango from the ballet *Façade*, other Sadlers Wells ballet members, and opera singer Joan Cross. Joan was a close friend of Benjamin Britten and a founder member of his English Opera Company. Caroline Shanks, Marion's playing partner and recent bridesmaid joined her on the piano in the first performance of Britten's *The Little Sweep*.

Marion was a keen supported of music in Yorkshire too. Princess Mary was the patron of the Leeds Triennial Music Festival and George was to become its Artistic Director from 1958 to 1974. In 1950, unusually for a society woman at that time, Marion was reported as being pregnant but intending to attend every night of the Leeds Triennial which that year featured a performance by Benjamin Britten.

Britten invited the Harewoods to come to Aldeburgh for a few quiet days of sea air saying that Morgan Forster was better but that it would do him good to be cheered up by a visit. George and Marion went to Aldeburgh in April that year and so began a series of many visits of the Harewoods to Suffolk and reciprocal visits of Britten and Pears to Yorkshire.

The letter of invitation ended by Britten saying how nice a chap Harewood was – gay, friendly and straight -

and congratulating the couple on the impending birth of their first child. "Love to you both – and I can't say enough how happy I was to hear the news the other day – in some stupid way I feel connected even with that! But perhaps I'm getting sentimental in my old age."[41]

The family maintained the royal connection and Marion with her husband and the Princess Royal entertained the new Queen Elizabeth, George's first cousin, with her husband Prince Philip. The young couples were of similar age. Marion and the Queen were both born in 1926, and mothers of small children. Despite their very different early lives, they had things in common and got on well. The Queen's sister, Princess Margaret came to stay too. George's mother Princess Mary became friendly with the Steins, particularly Sophie, Marion's mother, and Marion's parents often stayed at Harewood. There was a historical link between them. When Sophie was born in Mecklenberg-Strelitz, the Grand Duchess of that state was Augusta, a member of the British Royal family, a granddaughter of George III. When Marion married George, Princess Mary gave her many items of jewellery that had belonged to her great aunt, including a set of rubies. But apart from this background link, Sophie and the Princess Mary developed a close relationship. Whilst her husband Erwin's English was excellent, Sophie's was never very idiomatic. She had a way of muddling names, often referring to Peter as Ben and vice versa and once she called George 'Mrs Hurley', the name of the eccentric char-lady. When Marion was sometimes embarrassed by her idiosyncratic ways, Sophie would smile sweetly and say, "That is my sharm".

One famous malapropism recalled Marion, happened one night at dinner. Princess Mary always wore a long dress and her dachshund Punsch would be under her chair, covered by her skirt. "He let off a very smelly fart and Princess Mary jocularly waved her napkin to disperse the odour. Said my mother: "M'am, don't make such wind." Laughter all round and no offence taken."

As well as family occasions there were many weekend parties, just as before the war. But now the guests were predominantly from the world of the arts. The names of playwrights, actors and actresses, opera singers and conductors appeared in the visitor's book. There were many concerts and the family gave receptions for occasions such as the Leeds Music Festival, of which Lord Harewood was director. Although this life was new to Marion and very different to her life in London, she was no shy or naïve young bride. She was used to being visible to the public, having been trained as a concert pianist, and she was a performer. She looked the part of a countess too. Slim and dark she wore the elegant clothes of the day well. Appearing at events she wore her small hats, gloves and jewellery as though born to the aristocracy. Hardy Amies was a friend and sent her his designs to wear. She soon adapted to speaking in public too and, with her husband, Marion helped to support local activities. She opened playing fields, attended regimental dinners, was seen at concerts, and visited shows. Of the latter, George commented that she was more at home at the Huddersfield Choral Society's annual Messiah, or at the Harrogate Flower Show than at an agricultural show, but she played her part.

The house in Orme Square too was the venue for many

visits, receptions and concerts. It was a house with rooms of a good size for entertaining. On 18 May 1953, less than two weeks before her coronation, Queen Elizabeth and her husband Prince Philip went to dinner with cousin George and Marion at Orme Square.

Three sons were born to the couple over the next few years. All the boys were born at George and Marion's London house in Bayswater. At Harewood, their Yorkshire home, a bedroom and dressing room over the library were converted into day and night nurseries. David Henry George, the eldest, arrived on 21 October 1950. Queen Mary went to see him just eight days after he was born, George only just making it back to the Orme Square to see her as she had arrived early. Princess Alice, a granddaughter of Queen Victoria also wanted to see the new baby and arrived at the house unexpectedly with her husband Lord Athlone. George, who was walking back to Kensington with Erwin and Sophie, Marion's parents, reached their flat to receive a flustered message to say that visitors had arrived at Orme Square and had been shown up to Marion's bedroom where she was resting. George rushed back to find Marion and Princess Alice deep in a conversation about ration books.

Benjamin Britten agreed to be a godparent to David and was delighted with the prospect. The day after the birth, he sent a congratulatory letter to Marion.

"Because it'll probably be a few days before I can get to London to see you, I thought I'd scribble a few words to tell you how very very pleased I am about it all. Pleased that you are both well, that the son has good lungs (obviously going to be the Billy Budd baritone in a few years' time), but more seriously that you and George have a son. I could write reams describing my feelings on realising that you two whom I admire & love so much have this continuation, but since I can't write, it would only come out pompously in cliches, & so I won't say it. You know what I feel."[42]

Just four days later he wrote to George from Aldeburgh promising to go and see the baby as soon as possible. He says that he approves of the name David and "if a mere godfather has any sway in such matters, hope you'll stick to it" and ends by saying that his fishermen friends in Aldeburgh send respect and best wishes to Marion and the baby.[43] Britten soon fulfilled his promise and in November reported to his friend the conductor Norman Del Mar, that he has "seen Marion's babe quite a lot and he's fine. He's very gay." Just after Christmas 1950 Britten says that he is going up to Harewood for a few days holiday and combining it with the christening "of my newest godchild, David Lascelles." Once there he wrote to a friend that Marion is adorable with the baby – an excellent mother."

The christening of David Henry George Lascelles was on New Year's Day 1951. It was a local Harewood event, the tenants and villagers of the estate trudging through winter snow to the 15th century All Saints Church. Pathé and Movietone cinema newsreels of that week show the family after the christening, Marion and George look proud of their new baby viscount, now 13th in line to the throne. Maternal grandparents Erwin and Sophie are pictured too, along with Benjamin Britten as one godparent and the Princess Royal, who was standing in for another godparent, the baby's great grandmother Queen Mary, cuddling the baby.

Two more sons were born to the couple, just sixteen months apart: James Edward born 5 October 1953 and Robert Jeremy Hugh, known as Jeremy, on St Valentine's day, 14 February 1955.

The couple were very busy. Apart from the responsibility of Harewood House, the estate and a young family, George became highly involved in the musical life of Yorkshire and the country. In 1950 he was patron of the Yorkshire Symphony Orchestra's concerts and in 1958 he became General/Artistic director of the Leeds Triennial Musical Festival. He started the magazine Opera in 1950, became a director of the Royal Opera House Covent Garden from 1951, and in 1952 began to work there. He more than fulfilled his early ambition to work in the opera. He was also appointed a Counsellor of State, the only person to serve without being a Prince of the United Kingdom. He held the role from 1945 to 1951 and then again from 1952 to 1956.

Marion too was involved in the musical life of her husband and her friends, being an especial confidante of Benjamin Britten. The Aldeburgh Festival became an essential part of each year and although Marion did not play the piano in public any more, she was often Ben's trusted 'page turner' whenever he played in Aldeburgh. Through Ben she already knew many singers, librettists and musicians, many who had taken part in Ben's operas. Kathleen Ferrier was one such friend who had come into her life when Ben, with whom the Steins still lived at the time, was writing *The Rape of Lucretia* for her. Kathleen, from my own home town of Blackburn, had an irreverent sense of humour and delivered the most unrepeatable limericks, probably learned from her time as a telephonist. It was unlikely that she heard them at our joint alma mater, the staid Blackburn High School for Girls. Britten called her Rabelaisian; she took enormous pleasure in double-entendres, limericks, swearing, bawdiness, ribaldry and double-entendre jokes. Marion, at that time would have enjoyed Kathleen's company, she too enjoyed jokes and laughter, especially when she was not behaving in her Countess role. Kathleen was not at all impressed by George's title. One evening at dinner she and he had a heated discussion about their opposing views of a fellow artist. Afterwards she said, "I don't care who he's the Earl of, he wasn't going to get away with that."[44] Sadly this friendship between Kathleen and Marion was short-lived although remembered fondly by Marion fifty years later. Ferrier died in 1953 aged only 41.

It was not just friends that Marion made through her husband's work, her musical interests were fully engaged too. Although her husband had a professional role in opera, it was she who was a musician. Despite having given up her professional career on marriage, she had been part of the musical life of the nation since childhood. Britten often wrote to her with his concerns about his work and asked for her opinion. In 1950, for instance, when Billy Budd, one of his finest operas was occupying him.

"Billy is being quite a tyrant", he told her, "fascinating problems, difficult but rewarding. It is a strange business this, creating a world which finally ends by dominating oneself."[45]

On 4 March 1951 he wrote, "I long to play it to you and see how you feel." When *Billy Budd* was finished, Britten wrote to the Harewoods asking permission to dedicate it to them. In August that year he played the whole of the opera for Marion and George who thought that its emotional impact was comparable to *Othello*.

The couple were sometimes involved right at the beginning of a Britten project. In March 1952, Marion and George were on a combined music and skiing holiday in Austria with Britten and Pears. Their friends had already given two recitals in Vienna and they would go on to Wiesbaden for the German premier of *Billy Budd*. Between the recitals and the opera, the two couples drove to the ski resort of Gargellan near the Swiss border. In their hotel room, with George nursing a cold and Britten suffering from indigestion they began to discuss the operas they had seen and which of them exemplified a national mood. The conversation between the four developed into one about the absence of English 'national' operas, whereas other countries had them: *The Bartered Bride* for the Czechs, *Boris Godunov* for Russia, *Meistersinger* for the Germans and for the Italians, *Aida*. Britten decried this absence. "Well, you'd better write one," said George. By the end of the holiday the opera had been discussed and planned, even to who would be the best librettist, William Plomer. When George and Marion returned to London, George wrote to his cousin Tommy Lascelles, the Queen's private secretary, to suggest the opera as a perfect offering for the coronation which was due to take place the next year. The result was *Gloriana*, an opera based on the relationship between Elizabeth I and Essex, a distant ancestor of George, premiered at the royal Opera House during the coronation celebrations for Queen Elizabeth II. The first run-through of *Gloriana* was held at Orme Square, the Harewood's London home. A photograph from May 1953 shows Marion and George listening intently to the music. Just two weeks before the coronation, Benjamin Britten and his librettist, Christopher Plomer spent an evening at Orme Square with Queen Elizabeth and Prince Phillip, talking about *Gloriana*. Pears and Joan Cross sang parts of the opera to Britten's accompaniment. Joan Cross said later that it had not been an easy evening. "I don't think *they* enjoyed the evening any more than we did."[46]

It was not only music that occupied Marion and George. Marion had a real thirst for travel and a talent for planning it. As well as the visits to Suffolk to see Britten and Pears, where they enjoyed the music, fishing trips and walking, they took many journeys away from Britain. Only a few months after they married the couple went to Vienna, where Marion was born. It took three hours to fly there from Northolt, a military airport used as a civil airport until nearby Heathrow was completed in 1954. Reaching the city of Vienna, they saw ample evidence of the three occupying powers as well as the scars of combat. They often ate, usually very well, in cellars that had been patched up after the bombing. In the five years since the war ended, there had been a post-war boom of the Vienna Opera and in 1950 most of the company were still performing there, not having yet dispersed to other opera houses across the world. Ljuba Welitsch, a fine operatic soprano famous for her Salome and a key member of the Vienna State Opera, took over the entertainment of Marion and George during their visit. She knew George having met him when the company visited London in 1947, had sung Verdi's *Requiem* at the Leeds Festival and been entertained at Harewood. Bulgarian by birth she had taken Austrian citizenship in 1946 and was keen to introduce the young couple to Viennese customs. One night there was a visit to an inn at Grinzing for *Heurige,* where tender boiled meat accompanies the new white wine of the region. George had to insist that he and Marion took a walk before going to bed to recover from the potent wine. There were plenty of such social occasions and by the middle if the holiday, Marion, who spoke fluent German, complained that she had a sore throat, due less to the cold weather than from "rattling the guttural Viennese 'r' round her throat so often."

The fortnight was a great success. They saw *Turandot, Aida,* Britten's *The Beggar's Opera* and 'a splendid' *Meistersinge*r. "The only blots on our operatic map were a disappointing *Figaro* and the fact that there were no performances for the last four days of our visit due to a strike – I had never then (poor innocent) heard of a strike in the theatre."[47]

On this first visit Vienna, George became more familiar with Marion's home city of Vienna, both through its music and art. For Marion it was both a revisiting of childhood memories but also an introduction to a city changed by war. But for George, it was also an introduction to a very 'foreign' way of life.

"We were not in the simple tourist category; foreign because everything, from the overheating in the buildings to the *plumeaux* on the beds, from the plants in the living rooms to the formality and hospitable warmth of the inhabitants' behaviour, from the cosiness of restaurants to the central position occupied by the Opera, was foreign to my English upbringing – foreign but by no means unattractive."[48]

For the next ten years Marion and George travelled widely. Having a nanny for the children, which must have seemed a luxury for Marion at first, made it possible to be a mother, to travel and to play her role in the community. Many of the couple's trips were to Europe to the great opera houses of Paris, Milan and Vienna and to music festivals such as Florence. Marion met many of the greatest singers, musicians and conductors of the day, a great number of whom were to become personal friends and who she met often on their reciprocal visits to Britain, to perform in London, in Leeds, in Edinburgh, at Aldeburgh and at Glyndebourne. Through her husband's connections they were entertained on their travels by members of the European aristocracy as well as famous names in the opera world. Particularly memorable was a visit to Siena in 1950 after being in Florence for the Maggio Musicale Fiorentino. There they were entertained by Count Guido Chigi Saracini, an Italian patrician, composer, and musical patron. Marion and George slept with a Botticelli above the bed in the main guest room. Just 'a 'school' picture, explained the Count.

A second visit to Vienna in 1952 to see Alban Berg's widow was of particular interest. She understood no English but Marion had known Helene since she was a child and her own ease with the language meant that the visit, where Helene referred to her husband as though he was present, was made memorable for George.

George calculated that by the time the couple went to India for the first time in 1958, nine years after they married, they had made just short of fifty journeys out of England. Some of these journeys were in the company of Benjamin Britten and Peter Pears, and when Marion was pregnant and could not travel, George took at least one trip with Erwin, Marion's father, of whom he was very fond. In 1950, when Marion was expecting David, the two men went to Salzburg. Erwin was, as George recalled in his memoirs, "a rewarding travel companion, suffering with no apparent impatience my musical naiveties and able to share in my enthusiasms."[49] It was during this visit too that Erwin was recognised by a man who addressed him as 'Herr Chormeister' The man had been a member of Erwin's choir in Vienna before the war and Erwin was moved to reminisce with him about Schoenberg, Berg and Webern.

Many of Marion and George's activities and occupations were connected with a shared passion for music, and travel was often a way of experiencing the best in concert and opera performances. But they had other things in common too. They had three small boys who they both loved and a busy social life in both the north and south of England.

But perhaps common interests and much-loved sons were not enough. Their courtship had been short and once they were engaged, had been played out in public. They had not had a lot of time to get to know each other well before they married.

In his autobiography George mentions that by the late 1950s, problems between them had grown. Marion had accused him of sheltering behind a gramophone and typewriter and refusing to communicate with her on vital issues. A friend had told her, much to her understandable annoyance, that she did not come up to George's expectations of efficiency in running Orme Square and Harewood. Another friend had said that both parties were insufficiently tested by life and found it difficult to cope with anything that went wrong in an untroubled existence. Friends, however, are always wise after the event and Marion's version of that time is not available, but there were some signs that the couple were drifting apart.

In 1958 too, the year that Marion and George went to India, Erwin Stein, Marion's beloved father died unexpectedly, in July from two quick strokes. He was 72. There was an outpouring of grief from those who knew him. Benjamin Britten was devastated by the loss of his mentor and very close friend. The day after Erwin's death he wrote to Erwin's widow Sophie:

"I feel absolutely dazed, as if an anchor in these stormy days were taken away from me…. Twenty years! – I must always be grateful that I had the luck & privilege to know Erwin so long, & through such, for me, important years. He was so wonderfully understanding, so clear sighted, & yet so warm & enthusiastic."[50] Britten's final tribute to Marion's father, his great friend and colleague was a memorial concert on 30 January 1959 when he conducted the first London performance of *Nocturne*, "A ghostly thread running through Stein back to Mahler himself.[51]

On the same day he wrote to his good friend Princess Margaret (Peg) of Hesse and Rhine, a friend he had met through Sophie, to tell her the news about Erwin and his concern about how Sophie would cope, but added "Marion, of course, with so much of her father's security of character, is a marvel, & holding everything together." This strength of character, the ability to cope with whatever life offered, was perhaps partly inherited from both Erwin and Sophie but also a result of having to adapt at quite a young age to a new life. It would stand her in good stead in the years to come.

George Lascelles had been close to Erwin. He liked him as a warm and kind father-in-law but also respected him for his musical knowledge and skills. Erwin could be relied upon to offer sound advice. It was perhaps fortuitous that Erwin did not live to see the situation between his daughter and son-in-law that developed the year after his death.

SEVEN

The End of an Era

Benjamin Britten's letter on the 5 January 1959 to his friends the Harewoods wished them well for the year to come. "It was lovely being at Orme Square for the beginning of the New Year. How I hope it brings for you & Marion, & all the family, great happiness & satisfaction in every direction."[52]

But the wished-for happiness was not going to be. Only a few days later, three chance occurrences led to an event that totally changed Marion's life for ever.

In early January 1959, her husband was at the Air France terminal in Milan on the way back to London. George who had for many years been entranced by Maria Callas and her singing voice, had been to Milan hoping to persuade her to revisit London to sing in the opera that summer, and was disappointed that she had refused. Normally he would travel home directly from Milan to London.

However, the forecast was for fog that day, so he decided to fly to Paris and spend the night there rather than risk waiting for a direct flight which could be delayed, to be sure of reaching London the next morning.

In the waiting room with him was an attractive young woman carrying a violin case. This was Australian Patricia Tuckwell, en-route from Trieste to Paris. She too should not have been there on that day. She should have left France three days earlier. But a friend's illness had delayed her.

And unusually, there were only two people in the waiting room. Had there been many, the chances of the two meeting and talking would have been slim.

The Earl and Patricia Tuckwell chatted as they waited. Patricia was an Australian, a model in her youth and known as Bambi because of her long, slim legs. She was an accomplished professional violinist and at only sixteen she had joined the first violins at the Sydney Symphony Orchestra. Previously married and with a young son, she was by 1959 a single woman again. George did not know her but finding that she was the sister of Barry Tuckwell, who had become the most noted French horn player after the legendary Dennis Brain had died in a car crash in 1957, there was a musical connection. He knew and had met Barry. When the flight was called, George offered to carry the violin but Patricia would not part with it. She allowed him to carry her suitcase instead. They sat with each other on the plane and chatted. Since both were to be in Paris a few days later, George to see and hear an opera singer on behalf of Covent Garden, he invited Patricia to see *Salome* with him.

At home, George told Marion about his chance meeting with Barry Tuckwell's sister, Patricia. The same age as Marion she seemed to be an interesting new friend for both

George and his wife, and Patricia went to several plays and operas with the couple. In March, George, dressed in drag as the Ellen Orford character from *Peter Grimes* danced at the Opera Ball with Patricia, who had borrowed her costume from Marion. But the visits as a threesome were not the only times George had seen Patricia, he had seen her several times in London that winter without Marion's knowledge. Soon after the ball George told Marion that he had fallen in love. This was the start of a very difficult period for Marion. She must have been both angry and hurt. She had befriended Patricia and socialised with her. However Marion did not believe that the relationship would last and she was determined that her own marriage would survive. She hoped, and believed, that Patricia would get bored and return to Australia. Although Marion knew that her husband was seeing his new love frequently during the summer of 1959, she clung on to the idea that the relationship was transitory.

Unlike George, Patricia was a free agent, her previous marriage to a photographer had ended and she had a son, Michael, in his `teens, who lived with his father at home in Australia. She was perturbed by the situation, bothered that she was causing distress to Marion and aware that there were children to consider. So, late that summer, she decided that she would end her relationship with George and return to her life in Australia after continuing the round-the-world trip that had been interrupted by her affair. George was devastated at the thought of losing her and would not accept that she was moving out of his life.

George and Marion continued their activities as a couple despite the worsening situation. As the holiday had been planned long before, George and Marion went to stay with Igor Markevitch,[53] the Russian composer and his wife Topazia, near Positano. It must have been so hard for the couple to keep up the pretence of a stable and happy marriage in front of their friends as George was desperate to get back to London and to read the letters that Patricia had promised to send him there, care of Covent Garden. She wrote to say that returning to Europe would be folly and painful for everyone concerned. She had decided to stay and resume her life in Australia. But George was in love. This was not the passion of a young man but that of a mature thirty-six-year-old who wrote back to say that he could not contemplate the future without her. He spoke to Patricia on the phone and said that if she would not come to him, he would go to Australia and stay until she relented. This letter had the effect George wanted. A few days later Patricia wrote to say that she was resolving her business in Australia and would be with him by the beginning of 1960.

In the autumn of 1959, George told Marion the situation; that Patricia was coming from Australia to join him. According to George, Marion refused to take it seriously and doubted that Patricia would return to England. With three young boys of nine, six and four she must have been fearful of what the future held and preferred to believe that what George had planned would not happen. By the end of 1960, Benjamin Britten was aware that the happiness that he had wished for his friends the Harewoods in his New Year greeting had not materialised. He was cross at the conduct of his old friend George Lascelles and at how it was affecting his even older friend, Marion. Despite his own relationship with Pears, one illegal at the time, he had traditional morals and considered loyalty an essential virtue. On 13 April 1960 he wrote a warning letter to Roger, the 17-year-old son of Ronald Duncan, another of his friends, who had recently been staying with the Harewoods.

> "I wish people would think of the result of their actions. I am also rather worried about you, old boy, worried lest you think that this kind of sexual laxity is the way most of the world behaves, or should behave. But I do know (I really do know) quite a lot of happily married couples, with plenty of imagination and sensitivity (& desires) who manage to live together happily, in spite of, I am sure, problems from time to time."[54]

Increasingly, Britten would see more of Marion and less of George as the marriage foundered. For the next few years, the couple lived strange lives. George spent much time in London at the house in St John's Wood he shared with Patricia, visiting Harewood on his own. The new couple travelled about as a way of being together. George had been appointed Artistic Director of the Edinburgh Festival and despite adjusting to his changing marital situation, he remained professional in his work and was busy planning his first festival in 1961. He had chosen, after a project to foreground Schonberg had fallen through, to mount a retrospective of the sculptor Jacob Epstein. Four large pieces, essential to the exhibition were, unlikely as it seems, in Madame Tussauds wax museum in Blackpool. The only way George could have them for Edinburgh was if he bought them. Although they were very expensive, Jack Lyons, a Leeds business man and friend of the Harewoods who was interested in the Arts, agreed to pay half. George found the rest of the purchase price and the four statues of Genesis, Consummatum Est, Jacob and the Angel and Adam were bought from Tussauds and displayed in the then empty Waverley Markets in Edinburgh. At the end of the festival, all the pieces except Jacob and the Angel and Adam were sold off, Jack Lyons kept Jacob and the Angel and George the Adam. Epstein's monumental statue moved into the stables at Harewood and was displayed there. Later, in the 1980s, he was moved into the Hall at Harewood House, and is still now a powerful welcome to any visitor. "There he has stood for most of forty years, giving my wife and me immense pleasure and satisfaction every time we pass him on our way in and or out of the house," wrote George much later. What happened at Harewood at that time was increasingly less important to Marion than her life in London, and it is more likely that George talked to Patricia about his project rather than to his wife.

Marion persisted in refusing a divorce. She was still the Countess of Harewood however and although she spent more time in London as her marriage failed, she visited Harewood when her husband was elsewhere. She did not lose her links with Yorkshire. She had friends and interests there. And Harewood was, of course, the home of her boys and their inheritance.

The Russian cellist, Mstislav Rostropovich, Slava, who was a close friend of both Marion and Britten wrote about a visit that the friends made to Harewood during this time. After an Aldeburgh Festival, most likely in 1961,

Slava, Ben and Marion were driving north to Miki Sekers' Rosehill theatre in Whitehaven, Cumberland, where Ben and Slava were going to give a recital. They planned to stay the night at Harewood House. As the Princess Royal would be there, Slava was anxious to know how he should address a princess and was convinced he should curtsy. Despite the others telling him it was quite the wrong thing to do, he insisted on practising his curtsy on the high street in Aldeburgh before they left. When they stopped in Lincoln on the way to Harewood, Ben realised that Slava still intended, or at least he pretended he did, to curtsy to the Princess. Slava had wicked sense of humour and would have enjoyed his friend's consternation. Ben offered to do anything if Slava would not do it. Slava said "then will you write me six unaccompanied cello suites in return for my agreeing not to curtsy?" Ben agreed and the contract was drawn up on the back of a hotel menu.[55] Any offence to Princess Mary who was knitting when Slava arrived, was averted. Just half of the cello suites were written before Ben died. The 'contract' is now buried with other papers in the foundation stone of the Britten Theatre at the Royal College of Music.

By that year, 1961, things were increasingly strained between George and Marion although she was still refusing to accept George's relationship with Patricia as permanent. Maintaining the outward appearance of a happily married couple, they went on a visit to Japan on a scouting mission for the Edinburgh Festival, of which George was Artistic Director. Unusually, they took their eldest son, ten-year-old David with them. Both on the way there and back they stopped off in India, staying in some splendour at the

British High Commission and meeting Indian performers that his father was interested in bringing to Edinburgh. In his recent book, *A Hare Marked Moon*,[56] David looks back at that time and the reason his parents took him along.

> "Maybe they thought travel would broaden my mind. Perhaps it was because their marriage was in trouble…. And my presence meant they were not solely in each other's company. I had no idea about any of this at the time."

The trip to India did nothing to relieve the tensions in the marriage, but it did have one long lasting result. It sowed the seed of David's interest in the Himalayas and particularly Tibetan Buddhist culture which led to many travels there and the eventual building of a stupa in the grounds of Harewood; a project he writes about so colourfully in his book.

By 1964, Marion's marriage was obviously irretrievable. That July Patricia gave birth to George's son, Mark. The pregnancy had been a planned one, the couple deciding that if they wanted a child together it would be best to have it soon as Patricia was nearly thirty-seven. This age does not seem particularly old when viewed from the 21st century when many children are born to mothers well over forty, but it was more so in 1963. The reasons for having a child were probably more complex than just Patricia's age. George would realise that if he and Patricia had a child together it must signal to Marion and everyone else, that their relationship was permanent. Friends of George, or those he considered friends at the time, told him he had been trapped. In his autobiography however, he is adamant that the new child was what they wanted as there seemed little chance of marriage as Marion still refused to contemplate divorce. For his wife this was the ultimate betrayal. She was extremely hurt and angry. There was no way she could go on pretending that her marriage might survive. In Edinburgh 1964, there was a further scandal. Harewood's affair was no secret among the annual Edinburgh Festival caucus and Patricia was at the festival, as was Marion. When the Harewoods went back to see an artist after a concert, "Marion, seeing Patricia Tuckwell there, slapped her face with much invective in front of everyone present."[57] It was a rare occasion when Marion lost her cool and behaved instinctively. She was, although she managed to hide it behind a formal façade when necessary, a very passionate woman. She was extremely angry about her situation and for once, her feelings had been on show. After this incident, although not officially as a direct result, George lost his position as the director of the Edinburgh Festival and resigned as Chancellor of the University of York. John Calder, the writer and publisher who reported that incident says that his then wife, opera singer Bettina Jonic was firmly on Marion's side in the break-up, as were many women. Bettina was a friend of Marion's and involved with her in London's artistic and musical life. Friends were beginning to be forced into making choices about who they would support. It was not going to be easy to remain on good terms with both Marion and George.

It was shortly after this that George, realising that Marion would not give him an amicable divorce, decided to leave Orme Square for good. Having told Marion of his intentions, the couple planned how to tell their boys. The night before he left, Marion and he had a mutual exchange of thanks for the good things of their marriage; an exchange that George guiltily felt was better expressed on her part than his. He told his sons he was leaving Marion, and the next day waved his family off on a holiday, which was really a goodbye to the life he had known with them. They would always be his sons, but the future for all the family would be different. Inevitably life for the boys would change, especially for David, the eldest. In November 1964, David's cello teacher wrote to Marion saying that he thought it best not to continue with the lessons as it was painful to see David try to control his anger. There must have been more than a dislike for cello lessons to produce such anger in a fourteen-year-old. And a letter from Westminster school at about the same time reported that the school had struggled with the boys, but that things were getting better.

Marion contacted her friend Ben to tell him about the impending break. In a letter 28 July from Britten to his partner Peter Pears wrote that "The Harewood thing has now come to its inevitable dreary climax – all very sad & infuriating (The Children are being told this weekend.)" Britten had decided that his loyalties lay with Marion and that he could no longer be friends to both parties. In his autobiography, George recalled, sadly, how his long relationship with Ben ended. He had gone to the 1964 Holland Festival at a different time than Marion and after a concert at Scheveningen which Britten was conducting, he went to the dressing room to see Ben and Peter, only to see them push out past the queue, ignoring him. When he got back from London there was a 'curt' note from

Britten ending their association due to George's behaviour to Marion. Marion herself, to her credit, knowing how much the friendship of her husband and Ben was not only due to her but through their shared musical interests, tried, unsuccessfully to persuade Ben not to break with George. However, in January 1965, George's presidency with Aldeburgh Festival, a post he had held since the first festival in 1948, came to an end. Britten wrote:

> "My dear George, I hate to write this letter. Although our paths have recently gone in different directions, I often think of you with admiration and affection, and with gratitude for your very timely support at the early stages of our enterprises and of the many occasions on which we have both worked together on the things we have both believed in. All the same, we must face facts, & that it doesn't seem possible, at any rate for the time being, for you to come to our Aldeburgh Festival. Do you think, therefore, that it makes any sense your continuing to be our President? People are already beginning to notice your absence, & will soon begin to ask questions. If you agree with me, would you please just write a line of resignation to Fidelity Cranbrook? Yours, with sincere regret, Ben.[58]

Britten was known to dump friends and acquaintances suddenly without discussion if they ceased to be of use to him or if they offended him in some way. Conductor Sir Charles Mackerras was dumped for joking that the number of boys in *Noyes Fludde* must have been a delight for Britten. George Lascelles had coined the term "Ben's corpses" for such people and now he was one of them. Marion, on the other hand was a close friend to Britten and was always in favour.

Although George and Ben occasionally talked on the telephone about practical aspects of Britten's work, the friendship was never renewed. In the 1970s, Lord Harewood and Patricia visited Aldeburgh and talked briefly to the ailing Ben after a production of *Alceste* at Snape Maltings. But Britten was Marion's friend. When she and her second husband were climbing the stairs, also to visit Ben after the performance, Marion saw the Harewoods with Ben and promptly turned round again.

It was an acrimonious divorce. Marion was devastated and felt betrayed as her marriage drew to its close. She was intensely loyal herself to those she cared for and expected others to be so too. This meant that she expected her friends to take sides and take her part, a difficult decision for many. Britten obviously chose to support her, and to George's immense sadness ended a close and valued friendship. But others wanted the best for both George and Marion. Many letters from 'Aunt Madge', George's great aunt, his father's sister, express how much she cared for both parties.

> "I am sorry for both of you darling – and for George because what has come upon him is not all ecstasy"
>
> "I just go on praying that the call of loyalty and the background of Christian principles which must still be deep down within him will prevail and will induce him to fight what is going to make his nearest and dearest relations so miserable."[59]

Topazia Markevitch, a close friend to both Marion and George resolutely refused to break off friendship with either. Other friends did not want to take sides but were aware that they might lose Marion as a friend if they continued to see George. One who had been invited to Harewood for Christmas wrote to plead with Marion not to think she was disloyal if she went to stay, and not to drop her as a friend.

George had few friends with whom he could discuss his feelings about Marion, Patricia and his sons. His mother Princess Mary did not help him. She disapproved of his new relationship and refused to discuss the situation. Although she and Marion were not particularly close, living at Harewood with George and his wife, she had been only too aware of the increased time the couple spent apart from each other and of the open secret of her son's new relationship. Concerns for this situation were internalised by the Princess, she would not talk about them to anyone. Her husband Harry in whom she would have confided, was no longer alive. Such concerns began to affect her health so she had suggested in 1963 or 64 that for medical reasons she should leave Harewood and move south, perhaps to be near Sandringham which she loved. George suspected that her reason was more to get clear of Harewood before Mark's birth and the ensuing scandal than his mother's health. Her latest grandson was born about nine months before Princess Mary died, and of course she knew about him. but she would never have raised the subject. "We talked about him only once, and she received what I had to say in total silence and made no comment of any kind, except to ask, on the subject of a divorce, 'What will people say?'" [60] It is interesting to note that at that time too, George's brother Gerald was experiencing a similar marital dilemma. His marriage to Angela Dowding in 1952 had failed as Gerald met and fell in love with Elizabeth Collingwood. She too gave birth to a son, Martin, in 1962. The public did not know about this until 1978 when Gerald and Elizabeth were married in Vienna after Gerald's divorce. The Princess Royal never knew about Gerald's second family. She died suddenly on 28 March 1965, walking round the lake at Harewood with her son James and two of her grandchildren. George did not take Patricia to Harewood until after her death.

Some eighteen months after George left her for Patricia, Marion accepted the inevitable and agreed to a divorce. She would no longer be the Countess of Harewood. Apart from the loss of her husband she would lose her lifestyle and, perhaps more importantly for her, the ability to support things she believed in, often music-related, that her status as a countess had facilitated.

In January 1967, aware that press interest was putting immense pressure on all concerned, George, advised by his friend Ronnie Duncan, instructed his lawyer to send a press release.

"We have recently, on Lord Harewood's behalf, accepted service of divorce proceedings, whereby Lady Harewood's petitions for divorce on the ground of her husband's adultery with Miss Patricia Tuckwell. Lord Harewood will not defend these proceedings and he and Miss Tuckwell would wish to marry if and when they are legally free to do so. Lord Harewood has lived separately from Lady Harewood for the last sixteen months at his house in St John's Wood, London. A son, Mark, was born there to Miss Tuckwell in July 1964, of whom Lord Harewood was the father."[61]

Marion was granted a decree nisi in April 1967.

This did help to dampen down press interest although reporters continued to lurk around Hamilton Terrace where George and Patricia lived. A few months later, Marion generously agreed to allow David, James and Jeremy to meet their little half-brother, Mark. The boys got on well – there were now four young Lascelles siblings

That July, Marion and George's divorce, a decree absolute, came through, the first in the royal family in modern times. This divorce of the Queen's first cousin from his wife was big news for the press. The Daily Telegraph, not usually a gossip newspaper, had printed Mark's birth certificate showing the father's name left blank and now published an article about the decline of moral standards in Britain. Royal divorces were unheard of in modern times and this was a 'first'. It would be another eleven years before the Princess Margaret caused a similar consternation when she and Antony Armstrong Jones parted.

The queen's consent to George's remarriage, which was needed, was given at the Privy Council in July 1967. The Council's announcement stated:

"The Earl of Harewood has sought the Queen's consent, in accordance with the Royal marriage Act of 1772, to marry Miss Tuckwell. The Cabinet have advised the Queen to give her consent and Her Majesty has signified her intention to do so."

It is difficult nowadays to think such a decision could be controversial, but as the Daily Mail of the 14 July reported, the consultation with the Cabinet "showed readiness to offer advice and that it is prepared to protect the Queen from controversy."

Although most divorcees could marry in a registry office, this was not possible for those covered by the Royal Marriages Act, which included the Earl of Harewood. Nor could they marry in church. After much confusion and last-minute organisation, George and his potential new Countess flew to America to marry in the summer heat of a New Canaan, Connecticut, garden. While George waited for assent to his divorce, besieged by the Press, Lord Drogheda, Chairman of the Board at Covent Garden gave him refuge the night before he flew to America. The couple flew back to London the morning after their wedding, and a day later drove up to Harewood. The new family settled in well to country life, Mark went to the village school and Patricia became a country loving honorary Yorkshire woman. She took to football, which as her husband said, was as well, as he loved the game and was the president of Leeds United. Unlike Marion, she was then the only chatelaine of Harewood, George's mother having died two years previously.

In the aftermath of the divorce and George's new marriage, Marion was viewed sympathetically by most people and she continued to be welcome at many events where she might meet royalty. In June 1967, Britten entertained Queen Elizabeth at his house in Aldeburgh when she was in Suffolk for the opening of the new Maltings Concert Hall at Snape. It was a very special occasion and Britten and Pears had had a new porch built on to the house in preparation for the visit. Marion was part of the small welcoming party and Queen Elizabeth, who particularly liked Marion, went out of her way to be kind to the newly divorced ex-countess. It would not be so good for Marion's ex-husband, the Queen's cousin. His divorce affected his professional as well as his social and family life. When David Webster was due to leave the role of Chief Executive of the Royal Opera House in 1970, Harewood wanted. the job and began lobbying for it. The Chairman of the Board, Lord Drogheda did not want George in that role for a whole variety of reasons. But the fear that the Royal family were so shocked by Harewood's divorce and might boycott Covent Garden if he was in charge, and that George was bound to spend too much time on his estates, near Leeds, were both used as excuses to avoid appointing him. An offer to appoint him to the ROH Chair role also came to nothing. Lord Goodman, Chairman of the Arts Council "called the palace and asked the Queen's private Secretary, Sir Michael Adeane, if H.M. would object to having her cousin as ROH chairman. The reply was that she would not mind, albeit expressed in a fashion that indicated no great enthusiasm for the appointment."[62] The Royal history of relationships with divorcees, of Edward VIII, George's uncle, who gave up his crown for Mrs Wallis Simpson and that of the Queen's sister Princes Margaret, who twelve years earlier had given up the divorced Group Captain Peter Townsend, were still remembered. George was out of favour at court and his adultery, divorce and his remarriage, all royal taboos, had immediate consequences for him. Although he played no active role within the Royal Family, he was the elder son of the late Princess Royal, and the Queen's first cousin. He became a pariah in royal circles. The doors closed quickly against him and they remained shut for many years. He was not invited to his uncle, the Duke of Windsor's funeral in 1972 (this really bothered him) nor Princess Anne's first wedding in 1973. However, there was some softening of the royal attitude when he and Lady Harewood were invited to a local dinner in honour of Queen Elizabeth II's Silver Jubilee in 1977. It was the first time that Patricia was presented to the Queen. After Princess Margaret's divorce from Antony Armstrong-Jones in 1978, it became difficult to continue shunning the Earl of Harewood and George and Patricia received an invitation to the wedding of the Prince of Wales to Lady Diana Spencer in July 1981. Subsequently, Lord and Lady Harewood were included in other formal events, and they also welcomed the Queen and the Prince of Wales, on separate occasions to Harewood House.

Marion, however, was now the ex-countess. She had lost the fight for her marriage. She was single, the mother of three teenage boys, and firmly based in her London home.

It was time to face the future.

THREE

EIGHT

Hiatus 1959-1967

But, kind reader, before moving on with Marion's life, let us look back for a short time. The period from 1959 to 1967 was a hard time emotionally for Marion, but a very active one. Although devastated by her husband's affair, she did much more than dwell on her sadness and new situation. From 1959 when she was first told of the new woman in her husband's life, to the time of her divorce, in no way did she leave the public stage. The knowledge of her husband's relationship slowly moved from an open secret among family and friends to becoming common knowledge and the source of gossip in Leeds and among her London set. Despite this, she carried on playing her role as the Countess of Harewood, fulfilling both her local responsibilities in Yorkshire and those in music. The strength of character remarked on by Britten and well-known to those who knew her, was needed like never before.

Her instincts were to fight for her marriage. As Benjamin Britten had said when she marred the Earl of Harewood, if there were problems, she had good friends who would stand by her "through thick and thin". This they duly did. Many took sides although for some years Britten managed to stay friendly with both parties. Marion poured out her heart to this man who was, to some extent, a brother figure and who she had lived with in her teenage years. At first, Ben listened to her husband too and Marion and George saw him both together and separately over the next few years. There were still some holidays together, visits to festivals, musical collaborations and many visits to each other's homes. It was 1964 before he finally severed his links with George, a great sadness to the Earl as he had enjoyed a musical relationship and a close personal friendship with Britten for many years.

We get a glimpse of how Marion and Lord Harewood dealt with their disintegrating marriage through some of Britten's letters to the couple and to others who knew them. In July 1959, George was becoming more and more convinced that his future lay with Patricia. He was seeing a lot of her but Patricia, aware of the difficulties the affair would create, was debating whether to go back to Australia for good. Marion was still convinced that the affair would not come to anything. Benjamin Britten was close to the couple and aware of the tensions. It began to upset him that they were not happy. On 24 July that year, Britten wrote to his partner Peter Pears of a stay with the Harewoods in their London home.

"I stayed with George and Marion – very tense &, I thought, worrying. But they both seem to feel the corner's been turned – which is certainly true in one way – but I hope the scars will heal."[63]

This turning point had indeed come, but the fingerpost was pointing in different directions for Marion and her husband. George was in love and determined to have Patricia in his life, Marion was equally determined that her marriage would survive.

Britten was aware that things had not improved when he wrote to his friend Lord Harewood from Venice that October. He was still supportive of George, who had been approached about taking the role of Artistic Director of the Edinburgh Festival, and wrote to say he felt that his friend would do a good job there. (Harewood eventually fulfilled the role from 1961 to 1965.) He is thinking 'a great deal' of George 'at this horrid time', and reminds him of 'how precious' he is to many people because of his musical activities and personality. He sends love to Marion and the children too.

By early 1960, although Marion and George were still together, friends such as Britten were aware that things were unlikely to improve. On 22 January 1960 Britten wrote to Prince Ludvig of Hesse and the Rhine, who had become a close friend.:

"I expect to see George and Marion this weekend & will do what little one can, but I feel the situation just too lowering & infuriating – I'm all for the neck-ringing alternative at the moment, but I expect I'm wrong![64]

Marion was still hanging on to her marriage and the possibility of its survival, but both she and the children were suffering. She was sharing those concerns with her close friend Britten. Although both she and George stayed close to the composer at this time, they began to go separately to events with him, or to visit him. By the spring, George and Patricia were together for much of the time although there had been no formal split and George still lived officially at both Orme Square and Harewood. A letter from Britten to a mutual friend, Roger Duncan, comments on the situation.

"You seem to have had quite a weekend with G. and P. (George and Patricia) and had to work hard into the bargain. I am of course very sorry for George, but, I fear much more sorry for M. & the children who are really having an endlessly agonising time. I wish people just occasionally would think of the result of their actions."[65]

Perhaps Britten was the closest friend who was sympathetic to both parties. He and Pears were still spending time with both Marion and George together despite the tensions; they all holidayed in Dubrovnik from 2-11 July 1962. And when Britten and Pears were performing in the 1961 Leeds Triennial in October 1961, they stayed with the Harewoods. But increasingly Marion's social and musical life diverged from that of her husband. In March 1963, she flew with Britten and Pears to Moscow for a Festival of British Musical Art organised by the British Council. The programme was offered firstly in Moscow where the visitors found time for sightseeing with cellist Mstislav Rostropovich and his wife Galina, later to become firm friends of Marion as well as Ben and Peter.

They then went on to Leningrad (St. Petersburg) to repeat the performances. It must have been strange for Marion to find that one of the other soloists accompanying Pears in *Serenade for tenor, horn and strings* was French horn player Barry Tuckwell, Patricia's brother.

Back at home Marion was coping with her disintegrating marriage. In October that year, shortly after she had been to the Soviet Union with Britten, she and the boys interrupted his planned ten days of 'peace and work' by an unexpected and unplanned visit to Aldeburgh. She needed to get away from the discomfort of her married life and seek the comfort and advice of her friend. However, on the night of November 22 1963 the couple, still officially together, hosted a party for their friend Benjamin Britten's fiftieth birthday, following an hour-long celebratory programme of discussion and performances of Britten's work on BBC's only TV channel. Whether by common consensus or the hosts' decree, remembered John and Myfanwy Piper, two of the guests, it must have been the only dinner party in the western world that evening that did not discuss or even mention the assassination of President John Kennedy, in Dallas earlier that day. It was to be Ben's night at Orme Square, and only his.

By 1965, Marion had accepted the inevitable end of her marriage. George had finally left home and was permanently with Patricia. Britten was very concerned for his friend. Marion's mother Sophie had died in October, just seven months after Princess Mary. and although Marion had never been quite as close to Sophie as to Erwin, she greatly missed her mother. To Elizabeth Mayer, his American friend in November 1965, Britten wrote,

"It has been a worrying sad year for us all, both publicly & privately – and is keeping it up right to the bitter end. We miss Sophie more than one could have imagined. But Marion is wonderfully strong and uncomplaining – she has gone on from strength to strength, only the children (because of temperament and tension) are problematic. Still, she has now bought a little holiday home for them here, on the sea at Thorpeness, & we shall see more of them & perhaps help a little - They are in, in time for Christmas."[66]

The 'little holiday home' was Galnockie, quickly re-named by Marion as 'Curlews', a pre-war villa on the sea front at Thorpeness, just a few miles north of Aldeburgh. Bought for around £10,000 and having four to five bedrooms, it was big enough to house the family and to entertain visiting friends. Although the house was intended for Marion and the boys once the divorce was finalised, officially, as reported in the Daily Express,[67] the house was bought by the Earl and Countess of Harewood. "It is right by the beach", Marion told the reporter, "It's not a very sandy beach, but there are sandy patches. It is a sort of place for weekends and holidays and easy to get to by train or by car. As you know we have several places and we go north of course, but we will spend holidays in Suffolk." She knew at the time of course, that Harewood House very soon would no longer be her home

Unlike her house in Orme Square, she furnished Curlews with modern 1960s furniture, much of it still in the house today. And of course there was a piano. The house was close enough to Aldeburgh to see a great deal of her close friends Benjamin Britten and Peter Pears. In 1957, in a house swap with one of their friends, the painter Mary Potter, Ben and Peter had exchanged their Crabbe Street house for The Red House. The 17th century farmhouse, just on the outskirts of Aldeburgh was a quiet place, surrounded by a large garden and a home where Ben could compose in its tranquil setting. Now with her own base in the county, Marion spent more time in Suffolk with the Britten-Pears circle.

At times both upset and angry about how her life was changing due to her husband's affair, she was, nevertheless, coping well. She was still the Countess of Harewood and needed to maintain, at least outwardly, her role in Yorkshire and wider society. Uncertain about her future and perhaps to distract herself from what was going on in her personal life, she began to re-engage with her own musical interests.

Invited to become the first President of the Friends of Covent Garden in 1961, she took on the role with enthusiasm. Her appointment coincided with a much more powerful change at the company, that of the appointment of Sir George Solti as Musical Director of the Covent Garden Opera Company who "entered the Royal Opera House like a cyclone, a whir of cosmic energy that brooked no resistance." [68] As in many other aspects of life in the early 1960s, opera was not immune to change. His ten years at Covent Garden, saw Solti introduce changes that raised standards there to levels comparable to the finest international opera houses. During his time there too, the company was recognised with the grant of the title 'The Royal Opera.' Another, although less momentous change at the opera company in 1961, although one which affected Marion more directly, was George's departure from the company that year to take up the Directorship of the Edinburgh Festival after being the right-hand man of David Webster, General Administrator of Covent Garden for some years. Perhaps, as her marriage was failing, it helped her decision to take on the offered position at Covent Garden, to know that her husband would be involved in new work away from London. Although Marion's role was mainly ceremonial, for sixteen years she attended most of the events run by the Friends and calmly and effectively chaired a fundraising committee for them. She supported many musical causes, holding charity events, often concerts at her house, to help fund the organisation. However, her interests were not only musical, and she had many friends and acquaintances who sought her help for different causes. Benjamin Britten was a supporter of Christian Action, founded in 1946 by a fellow pacifist, the anti-Apartheid campaigner Revd. Canon L. John Collins. The system of Apartheid, which denied non-white South Africans basic human rights, such as the right to vote sparked significant international and domestic opposition. Between 1960 and 1983, 3.5 million black Africans were removed from their homes and forced into segregated neighbourhoods as a result of apartheid legislation. Marion did what she could to help the cause. On November 18, 1960, with Canon Collins, she organised a charity concert at the Royal Festival Hall in London, in aid of Christian Action. She recruited her friends to help. Britten, Pears, Yehudi Menuhin and contralto Norma Procter performed a programme designed by Britten, which included works by Mozart, Purcell and

Bach. The programme explained that the concert was being held 'to support the Defence and Aid Fund administered by Christian Action', a fund raised to 'safeguard freedom and human dignity in Southern Africa without regard to Colour, Race, Creed or Political Affiliation.'

Music was, however, her abiding passion; she was especially interested in encouraging children to get involved. In the early 1960s she joined Ronald Duncan in editing an anthology of children's songs for the publisher Anthony Blond. Duncan too was a friend of Benjamin Britten, another fellow pacifist like Canon Collins and, like Britten, a successful conscientious objector in WW2. Marion and Duncan asked three composers, Britten, Francis Poulenc and Zoltan Kodaly if they would contribute to the book by setting Shakespeare's "Tell Me Where is Fancy Bred" to music. This they duly did, Poulenc dedicated his, rather oddly, to "Miles and Flora", the fictional children in Britten's opera *The Turn of the Screw*. It is hoped that the real children who would sing the song would not be affected by the sort of erotic fancy experienced by Miles and Flora in the opera. Britten asked permission from Ernst Roth, now his contact at Boosey and Hawkes after Erwin's death, to give the setting to Marion and Duncan.

"I have written the little song, which is not of great importance, and would like them to have it if you agree. I see no reason why B.& H. should not publish it later, if you felt inclined."

A revised version, retitled 'Fancie' was published by Boosey and Hawkes in 1965.

But Marion's much greater involvement in a music project started that year too. One morning in 1961, Fanny Waterman who was a well-known and highly regarded piano teacher in the Leeds area, rang her. Six years previously Marion had met Fanny at a tea party at the home of Lady Parkinson, a friend of Marion's mother-in-law, the Princess Royal. The two women shared not only their musicianship but a background of emigration. Fanny's father, Myer Waterman, another Jewish refugee, had left Russia for England at the turn of the century to be a jeweller. The family settled in England and Fanny was born in 1920. When Marion had wanted to arrange piano lessons for her son David, he became a pupil of Fanny's. Since then, Marion and Fanny had become firm friends. Marion and Fanny often played duets together and it was with Fanny that Marion played the one professional engagement of her life after her marriage; a BBC broadcast of works by Schubert, Ravel and Poulenc from a Leeds studio. Fanny Waterman always credited Marion as an unsung hero of music. She recalled in later life how famous musicians stayed at Harewood when visiting Yorkshire and how once, when Rubenstein was there, Marion arranged for four of Fanny's pupils to play for him. And Fanny remembered too how Marion and George's contacts in the musical world in the early days of the Aldeburgh Festival helped their friend Benjamin Britten to secure the best musicians to play and sing there.

Fanny Waterman had for some time been concerned about what she saw as the complacent attitude of far too many British institutions and teachers of the piano. Compared with the Soviet Union, the USA and some

European countries, teaching standards were low, and professional pianists were, she felt, consistently failing to match up to the level of their overseas contemporaries. She had the idea of an international competition for piano playing that would increase the standing of Britain and give young pianists something to aim for. But such a major competition would need organisation and funding. She would need help.

Her phone call to Marion came after Fanny had spent a sleepless night thinking about her project. Who better to help, she had decided, than her friend, the Countess of Harewood, who was herself a musician and had both social and musical contacts. As a presence in the community and an ex-professional piano performer she was the ideal person to approach. In an interview when she was in her nineties, Fanny remembered that by just saying that she was the Countess of Harewood, Marion could get support for the new venture. And when the two of them jointly mentioned it to influential people in the Leeds area, she was surprised at how many of them thought it a good idea. It would put Leeds on the cultural map. One of such people, a local Leeds businessman, Jack Lyons,[69] offered £1000 to help set up the competition and his wife Roslyn, a trained singer and active in her support for the competition, gave another £1000 for a first prize. Jack Lyons was a generous philanthropist, especially supporting the arts in his home town of Leeds and further afield. He had rescued the Leeds Musical Festival from closure in 1955 and brought in Marion's husband George as the festival's musical director. Lyons insisted that he should be the chair of the competition committee as he had donated such a large sum. Fanny Waterman who was really the obvious choice for chair, nevertheless agreed with his appointment, and she also agreed that Marion, whose social position was a great asset, should co-chair with Jack. She herself would support as vice chair. Although support from Leeds City Council was hard-won, the councillors eventually agreed to match Jack Lyons's contribution. The Arts Council of Great Britain and the Leeds Triennial Music Festival (under the directorship of Marion's husband Lord Harewood) weighed in with some financial support and many local businesses, banks and private individuals donated prize money. Princess Mary, Marion's mother-in-law became a patron and agreed to present the prizes. She contributed the Princess Mary Gold Medal for the winner, a medal which has continued to be awarded at every competition since the first, despite the princess dying in 1965. The University of Leeds too became closely involved, Fanny Waterman was a close friend of the then Vice Chancellor elect and his wife who was a keen amateur pianist.

Marion threw herself wholeheartedly into the project. Both she and Fanny had formidable organisational skills. Their committee set a date for the first competition, 13-21 September 1963, two years ahead. They secured a practice hall and some accommodation in the University. They arranged for the first two stages of the competition to be held in the University's Great Hall and the final stage in Leeds Town Hall. The Royal Liverpool Philharmonic Orchestra were booked for the final. Any of the city's residents with pianos were asked to volunteer to host overseas competitors. Marion and Fanny together personally selected the competition repertoire, including a compulsory piece at the second stage. At Marion's request, Benjamin Britten composed *Notturno* or *Night piece* for this, "a delicate, atmospheric work of subtle beauty, demanding great control of pedalling and interpretive skill – an ideal piece to sort out the musician from the mere technicians."[70]

The duo assembled an impressive group of well-known names for their first jury. Sir Arthur Bliss, the Master of the Queen's Music agreed to be the first chair; Hans Keller, a musician who wrote lively pieces for musical journals and who, like Marion had left Vienna in the Anschluss, was chosen as vice-chair. British jury members were John Pritchard, then musical director of the Royal Liverpool Orchestra and the Liverpool Philharmonic Orchestra, Clifford Curzon, Marion's former mentor, also a friend of Fanny's, and Paul Huband of the BBC. The only woman on the jury was the Polish pianist and teacher Barbara Hesse-Bukowska. Both Marion and Fanny had international contacts, Marion particularly so. She had spent many years with her husband, Britten and Pears visiting concerts and opera houses in Europe and beyond. She knew many people in the world of music.

Despite the Cold War[71], Soviet Union and British musicians had continued to reach out to each other, and Britten in particular, had developed close written friendships with both Rostropovich and Shostakovich, meeting the composer for the first time at the London premiere of the latter's cello concerto in 1960. Although neither Rostropovich or Shostakovich spoke English nor Britten Russian, they seemed to understand each other perfectly through what they called 'Aldeburgh Deutsch' and enjoyed a shared sense of humour. I found it a surprise to learn that Marion spoke Russian having chosen to have lessons as an adult, and was able to help translate communications that went back and forth between the three friends. She obviously had an aptitude for language, first shown by the speed in which she had learned English when she arrived in London from Vienna.

While in Moscow she was able to discuss the new competition with Madame Furtsova at the Ministry of Culture. She took advice from a range of Soviet musicians with various specialities, Chopin, Mozart, Bartok, twentieth century French music and the Classical repertoire. But her main coup was to secure the services of a great Soviet teacher and pianist Jakob Flier, a specialist in the Romantic repertoire, to sit on the first jury.

All was ready for the competition.

NINE

The first 'Leeds'

There were a few unforeseen hitches and problems at the first competition. Two members of the jury did not arrive when planned, and the second stage coincided with Yom Kippur which enraged Orthodox Jewish opinion in Leeds as two Jewish entrants were require to play on that day. There was also inevitable controversy when a local boy, Michael Roll, a pupil of Fanny Waterman won the final and took the first prize. Fanny remembered Marion walking down the stairs after Michael had played and saying to her, much to her consternation, as she had not expected it, "Michael was really good. He might win it." And Fanny also remembered Clifford Curzon, pianist, and Marions's old friend and musical mentor, kissing her and saying that Michael's rendition of Beethoven's Appassionata was the best he had ever heard. The win was well-deserved despite the initial complaints.

It was almost exactly sixty years after the first Leeds Piano competition of 1963 when I spoke to Michael Roll the classical pianist about his memories of Marion and of that first Leeds International Pianoforte Competition. He was the first winner and to this day the youngest at only 17.

Michael lived in Leeds and went to Roundhay school. Already a piano prodigy he had played in public since childhood. He remembered being described in a newspaper in one of his early appearances on stage as chubby and in shorts. He appeared with the City of Birmingham Orchestra at ten and at the Royal Festival Hall at twelve under the direction of Sir Malcolm Sargent.

Despite in 1963 not having decided on music as a career (he was seriously considering being a doctor like his father), winning the Leeds catapulted him into a playing career; one which in retrospect, he says, he would have liked to take more slowly. However he went on to a long, successful, and still-continuing life as a concert pianist. He has played with many of the great conductors: Boulez, Boult, Giulini, Haitink and Previn to name just a few. He has performed at all the prestigious venues, played at the last night of the Proms and travelled the world. Orchestras with which he has been associated, too many to mention them all, include the Boston Symphony with Sir Colin Davis with who he made his American debut in 1973. He is married to another talented concert pianist Juliana Markova

Whether he would have entered the competition at such a young age had he not been a Leeds boy and the pupil of one of the founders, is unlikely he thinks. He was not 'the finished product' and felt pressure that in retrospect was too great. However, Marion and Fanny were collecting potential entrants and there was a feeling of 'wouldn't it be great if Michael entered'. And so he duly did. He remembers being surprised and gratified to reach the final and his success was a real surprise. There was some opposition to his winning the competition as he was a local boy and there was a vociferous group who thought that the young Russian pianist Vladimir Krainev should have been the winner or co-winner. This was rather unsettling for Michael although the jury's awarded marks showed him to have won convincingly. He remembers walking along a road in Leeds during the competition and being hailed from the other side by the famous Russian pianist Jakob Flier, one of the judges that Marion had persuaded to take part. "Roll?" Flier called across, "Appassionata. Very good."

He met Marion at social events both before the competition and afterwards. He remembers being at the Festival Hall in London the year before the competition to perform for the Queen and Prince Philip. Marion and her eldest son David, four years younger than Michael, were there too. David was playing with a stack of wheelchairs used for the audience and Michael was in the hall for a rehearsal. Boys will be boys and Michael remembers being seated in a wheelchair and being propelled down the aisle of the Festival Hall by David, at breakneck speed.

Marion was elegant and 'queenly' Michael remembers. She was the Countess of Harewood as well as a founder of the Competition. She was warm and always the same. Her friend Fanny was not as consistent and Michael appreciated Marion's kindness. Fanny worshipped Marion and aspired to her social heights, he said. She changed her voice from her normal accent to a 'posh' one, he said, when talking to Marion.

Michael's Jewish parents, like Marion's, had left Vienna before the war although unlike Marion, Michael was born in the UK. The Jewish community in Leeds was very musical and there were musical evenings among many of the emigre households there. Michael says Leeds was a very gossipy city at that time and there were rumours of the rift between the Earl and Marion although it was 'hush hush' in public. There was a lot of dinner party talk about the Harewoods, which in 1963 Leeds was as interesting as the Profumo Affair in politics taking place at the same time in the South. [72] Marion managed to play her part in the delivery of that first competition with grace, not showing any of the internal turmoil that she must have felt at the time.

Both Marion and Lord Harewood were generous to young musicians and Michael was booked by George in his role as Artistic Director for the Edinburgh Festival of 1964, and recommended to the conductor Giulini. Famous visitors and performers at that festival included Marlene Dietrich, Yehudi Menhuin and Indian film stars who George had booked when he and Marion had visited India in 1961. Although only just 18, Michael was booked to play Mussorgsky's *Pictures at an Exhibition* at the Usher Hall; a video from the time shows him practising – and how talented he was. He remembers the scandal surrounding the Harewoods at Edinburgh that year, and that both Marion and Patricia were there. The Earl and Marion were such a glamorous couple that people could not believe that either one could stray.

Michael and Marion were further linked through Marion's friendship with Benjamin Britten. At the Aldeburgh Festival in July 1964, the still very young Michael played duets with Britten, including the great F minor fantasy. Ben insisted on the young Michael taking the more difficult upper part. Michael was concerned that his playing had not done the duets justice but Britten was charming, reassuring and helpful. He and Michael kept in touch. In 1974 Michael played Britten's piano concerto at the last night of the Proms with Charles Grove conducting, and went to the composer's home, the Red House just six months before he died in 1976. Britten sat and listened as Michael played through his piano concerto for him and "made some very pertinent remarks, always done with immense good taste and respectfulness – definitely one of the highlights of my career." Afterwards there was tea. Michael remembers a sunny afternoon, Britten ailing but hospitable, tea by the window and wasps invading the cakes, and Michael worrying that they might sting Britten.

Despite the early hiccups, the first Leeds Piano Competition was a great success, many now-famous performers having been successful in winning the 'Leeds': Radu Lupu, Murray Perahia, and Sunwook Kim among them. Marion continued to play a key role in the organisation and delivery of each triennial competition until 1983 when she resigned as she could no longer devote sufficient time to it. The Leeds International Piano Competition, or 'The Leeds', as it is familiarly known, goes from strength to strength with many patrons, early stages held internationally and the recitals beamed worldwide. A project which came as a welcome distraction to Marion at a difficult time in her marriage, is now recognised as one of her key contributions to the musical life of Britain and beyond.

In the late 1960s, now spending some time in London teaching the piano, she began another collaboration with Fanny Waterman, the success of which must have exceeded their wildest dreams. It was just luck, Fanny recalled in an interview in 2018.[73] One evening she and her husband Geoffrey were at Harewood for dinner. Other guests included Benjamin Britten and Peter Pears who were at Harewood preparing the *Winterreise* song cycles for a series of concerts there. Fanny was approached by a man she didn't know, who suggested she should write music teaching books. When he had gone, she turned to Ben to ask if she knew who the man was. The answer was no, but Ben suggested that his publisher Faber might be interested in such a project. She enlisted an enthusiastic Marion, and they began to write attractive, friendly non-stuffy primers for young pianists and for older beginners, the 'Me and My Piano' series. The two had great fun, including pictures and decoration to attract the young pianists, and making up rhymes with words that matched the rhythm of the music. They used to "laugh and laugh" said Marion. One rhyme was:

Monkeys climbing in the trees
Scratch themselves to catch the fleas.
If you see them in the zoo,
You may catch a flea or two.

Starting with one primer, Piano Lessons Book 1, published in 1967 by Faber, the series they started includes at least thirty titles for both elementary and intermediate grade pianists. The list is long and includes Piano Lessons, The Young Pianist's Repertoire, Two at the Piano, Piano for Pleasure, Monkey Puzzles Theory and Piano Playtime. Many of the titles have more than one book in the series and most have been re-issued and updated. The 'Me and My Piano' series is probably the most widely used and biggest selling piano method in the UK. The books have sold in their millions and have helped generations of young and not-so-young beginners to enjoy playing the piano.

Despite these musical distractions from the changes happening to her marriage, in early July 1967 Marion found herself once more a single woman and starting a new chapter in her life.

TEN

Starting Again

Divorced from George, and now just Lady Harewood, Marion was awarded custody of her three children. As part of the settlement, she would keep the house in Orme Square, north of Kensington Gardens, the house she considered as home. The house was not hers, but she had the right to occupy it for as long as she chose. The divorce settlement also gave her sufficient money to live comfortably. At only 40, she was the single mother of three bright lively teenagers who were more interested in the popular music of their generation rather than the classical repertoire she loved. She was living in the new world of 1960s 'swinging London'. She was no longer a countess. She would need all her reputed strength of character to build a new life.

Marion had been living apart from George for some years before she was divorced from him so the house in Orme Square was already the main home for her and the boys. It also became a home for many of the wider family when needed. After George left, Marion reorganised the house and created a flat in the basement. Her much older cousin Marie moved in after getting a job at Marks and Spencer's, the first job she had had in her life. Marie had a colourful past and Sophie disapproved of her but had taken her in. She had lived with Marion's parents in St. Johns Wood, in the maisonette they shared with Ben and Peter, after her marriage ended. Marion, always ready to help, offered her a home. After a few years at Orme Square Marie moved out to be with her new partner and the flat was available to others who needed help with accommodation in London. There was another apartment at the top of the house and a mews cottage which had its entrance on Orme Lane, the small road at the back of the big houses. After Erwin's death, Marion's mother Sophie lived in the cottage to be near her daughter. In August 1965, Sophie suffered a stroke while Marion and the boys were on holiday in Dubrovnik. She was in Aldeburgh at the time so Britten's sister Beth kindly looked after her until Marion returned. It was planned that Sophie would recover at the Orme Square house with Marion before returning to the cottage in Orme Lane when she was well. Lilia, a new helper who had just arrived from Portugal was to be her au pair. However, Sophie died in the big house on 2 October 1965. She was 82. Marion's close family was now just herself and her three sons.

According to her sons as they thought back to those times, day-to-day life did not change much after the divorce. The younger boys attended Hall School in Belsize Park until old enough for Westminster School where David was a weekly boarder. He came back to Orme Square on Saturday evening after afternoon sports and returned to the school on Monday morning. In his last year he became a day pupil. Marion's two younger sons became day boys at Westminster too. Some holidays were spent at Harewood although they often holidayed with people they knew in Europe. There was the trip to Dubrovnik to see many Yugoslav friends, and a remembered visit to an estate at Livorno in Tuscany with their mother and Lavinia, Tommy Lascelles daughter, and her two sons Nick and Simon. Visits to Curlews, Marion's base in Suffolk, saw them socialising with Britten's Aldeburgh music set and enjoying outdoor activities, swimming, boating and fishing. In London, the big house saw many composers, singers, conductors and other musicians come to stay. Boris Christoff the opera singer, conductor Giuliani and of course Benjamin Britten and Peter Pears were regular visitors

London was, in the late 1960s and early 1970s, as Marion's son James recalls, heaven; the place to be, particularly if you loved music. 'Swinging London' was the centre of the cultural revolution at that time. It was the home of Mary Quant's mini-skirt, the Kings Road and Carnaby Street fashion, political activism and sexual liberation. And the music! So much of it: the Beatles, the Rolling Stones, The Kinks, the Small Faces, and, as the next decade began there was Glam Rock with David Bowie, Elton John and Gary Glitter. Despite the political scene which became bleaker as the 70s progressed with 'Bloody Sunday' a mass shooting in Northern Ireland at the height of the 'Troubles' there, a miners' strike, and the chilly and dark three-day week to save electricity, it was nevertheless a good time to be young in London. All the boys had been introduced to music by their father and Marion from a young age, but this music was different. James started school at Westminster and on the first day he decided that he would stay for the next four years because his mother wanted him to and he did not want to disappoint her, but as soon as he could leave, he would start a band. Marion was totally supportive of his interest in music. It was not her music, but she would do whatever she could to help.

When, at about 12 or 13, James wanted to learn the drums, he started on the snare drum. But he wanted to make a much louder sound so a big drum kit was installed at the top of the house. Marion knew it was going to be noisy but accepted it and welcomed his friends to the house to play with him. Her many contacts in the music world came in useful too. Drum lessons were arranged with the distinguished percussionist Jimmy Blades.[74] Marion's close friend Benjamin Britten had met him in the 1935 when Blades played on the sound track of Britten's *Night Mail*.[75] The two men renewed their friendship in 1953 with Ben's call to Blades to play, at short notice, in a performance of *Albert Herring*. Blades made his mark immediately, and from then onwards he was a regular performer at Aldeburgh and the key percussionist for many of Britten's later works.

John Taverner, composer and organist, was just coming to prominence as a musician with his 1968 debut dramatic cantata *The Whale*, later released on the Beatle's Apple label in 1970. Marion thought that he would be able to help James with his urge to improvise in his music, and contacted him. James remembers this very tall figure with long hair and long spider-like hands coming over to see him. Taverner had the key to an orthodox church on Kensington High Street which housed a huge three-console organ. There was no-one there and after James had played a little rather self-consciously, Taverner encouraged James to start playing 'what you don't know' and the two of them banged the keys together with all the stops out. Anyone hearing the cacophony would have wondered what on earth was going on.

One group of visitors among many at that time to Orme Square, stands out in David's memory. Ravi Shankar, the Indian sitarist and composer had been a friend of his father and Marion since Benjamin Britten had taken them to an early sitar recital at the small Friends' House in Euston Road in the 1950s. The musician who, by the 1960s was famous, had been up to the Edinburgh Festival's Indian year in 1963, to improvise with Western musicians, guitarist and lutenist Julian Bream and harmonica player Larry Adler in particular. The Beatles too were influenced by Shankar's music. At the height of the Beatle's fame and fortune in the mid-nineteen sixties, George Harrison had begun a musical relationship with Shankar which influenced both his music and his spirituality. Marion said she did not really like the Beatles' sound; it was not her type of music. But she was persuaded by Ravi to go with him to see the film *A Hard Day's Night*. Ravi liked the company of beautiful women and Marion was certainly very attractive. After the film she changed her mind about the Beatles. Invited when in London some years later to visit Orme Square, Ravi arrived, to the astonishment of three teenage boys, with George Harrison and Paul McCartney.

Visits by those connected with the family and music

were part of Marion's life at this time. A well as caring for family members, the cottage belonging to the house, the top flat as well as the main house rooms were often occupied by visitors, some long-term. She held meetings of the organisations she supported in the house, musical evenings and concerts in the spacious rooms, creating events which were, albeit unknowingly, similar to the Viennese salons of her birthplace. There was always a grand piano in the house and Marion did not neglect her musicianship although she no longer performed professionally. She continued to write the volumes of piano teaching books and gave piano lessons, she listened to music all the time.

However, one of the things that surprised her sons was that although there was always music in the house and she had her Steinway in the music room, Marion rarely played music at home except for teaching and when preparing her teaching manuals, not much for her own pleasure and certainly not to entertain others. It was likely that had things been different she would have continued her career as a concert pianist. Jeremy, her son remembers speaking to George Martin, the famous record producer, about Marion. Martin was a contemporary of Marion, they were both born in 1926, and he had studied classical piano at the Guildhall School of Music at the time when Marion was starting her professional career. His time as a student had been delayed by war service. He had heard Marion play and was impressed by her musical ability. But perhaps by the time she was divorced and no longer had the role of countess to fulfil, she felt it too late to re-acquire her previous skills as a pianist. Or perhaps knowing so many famous musicians, she felt that there was no need for her contribution to the world of music as a performer, and that her role in music lay elsewhere.

Outside of her family, music continued to play the largest part in her life: helping young pianists, organising events, serving on committees, and attending concerts and operas. But it was not just the arts that she enjoyed. She was a good skater having learned long ago as a child in Austria. Just round the corner from Orme Square was the Queensway Ice Rink, still functioning today, and Marion and the boys would skate there on some Saturdays. When the free-for-all session ended and the younger people retired to the café with the juke-box, Marion would skate stylishly on the ice, once dancing with her friend Hardy Amies the fashion designer. She was a good swimmer and enjoyed skiing. Life was busy. As a beautiful and still young woman, she was no doubt in demand by suitors, but her sons say that whoever they were, she was most discreet.

When James left school, he did what he had always intended to do, he started a band. Marion bought him a huge Hammond organ which he said, looked like a drinks cabinet. And with this he toured with his band. The first band was based in a commune at Church Farm, owned by the Lascelles family, on the Suffolk coast, just five miles from the home of Peter Pears and Benjamin Britten. Pears supposedly complained about the band noise that disturbed his own practice sessions – probably as a joke. On the front of the truck the band used for a CND march to Aldermaston in 1972, was the label Global Village Trucking Company and the name stuck as a new name for the band. The "Globs" to its fans, was a rock group who wanted to make it without a record label or all the trappings that usually accompanied successful groups. By 1973 the group of about fifteen people, the performers, their girlfriends, children, and friends who acted as roadies and managers all lived together in a commune, based in a thatched cottage in Norfolk. By this time too, Marion's youngest son Jeremy had left school and joined the group, playing percussion with the band and acting as a roadie. The skills that would lead to his early career as a tour manager in the 1970s were soon developed. The band lasted until 1975, having recorded albums and played at benefits, free festivals, student protests and prisons. Both of Marion's younger sons went on to have continuing careers in music, James as a musician and Jeremy as a music executive at Virgin, then Chrysalis and more recently with his own company Blue Raincoat Company. He maintains his Yorkshire roots as a visiting professor of Music at Leeds College of Music, and also, like his brothers, is an ardent Leeds United supporter. Marion supported her boys and visited them at the house in Norfolk and went to band concerts when she could. The music they played was not the classical music loved by Marion or their father, but she accepted their choices and welcomed the new experiences and new people she met though them.

David, Marion's eldest son, also developed a career in the arts, but not in music like his brothers. On leaving school he lived in the West Country for many years and since the early 1980s he has been a film and television producer. His early films reflected his love of travel, later work was in both film and television including producing nine episodes of the highly successful Inspector Morse and the TV series The Fortunes and Misfortunes of Moll Flanders.

He became the 8th Earl of Harewood in 2011. Marion must have been very proud of her three sons. They were all, in their different ways, making their way in the world. There were an increasing number of grandchildren to love. Her family role in the future would be as a grandmother rather than a hands-on mother.

Or would it?

FOUR

ELEVEN

Jeremy

As now Lady Harewood, single again and living permanently in London, Marion was welcomed in musical circles. She had music credentials, being recognised as being involved in a variety of projects including the Leeds Piano Festival, teaching primers, Covent Garden and Aldeburgh, and she knew many of the famous conductors, musicians and singers of the day. There were plenty of operas, concerts and festivals to engage her attention, plenty of friends to support her. The next few years were busy ones. She spent much time in Suffolk with her Britten-Pears set and with Ben and Peter welcomed Queen Elizabeth II on her visit to Aldeburgh in June 1967. She travelled in Europe and to the Soviet Union. Friends who she entertained in her London home included cellist Mstislav (Slava) Rostropovich, Boris Christoff the famous bass, violinist Yehudi Menuhin and many more. By the early 1970s, Marion's sons were young men leading their own lives and she was able to think about her own future. She began slowly to regain her cheerful personality, her reserve less in evidence. She enjoyed smoking, her 'Bloody Mary' cocktails and her social life as a newly free woman. One feature everyone who knew her remembers about Marion was her interest in all and everything. She was open-minded and would support friends and family in everything they did, even though it might not be what she thought she would enjoy. She opened her mind to music of all kinds and from different parts of the world, and theatre and literature. She was delighted for instance, to welcome musicians from a visiting Mongolian orchestra to stay at Orme Square.

As well as her commitments with the Leeds Piano Festival and writing what were to become a constant flow of music primers, she helped friends where possible and supported many causes. She sent a letter of introduction to Charlie Chaplin when Britten wanted to show his films in Aldeburgh, she translated Rostropovich's letters for Britten and met the composer Shostakovich when she visited the Soviet Union, taking along messages from Britten and sending him the Soviet composer's responses. At home in London, she had a busy social life. Musical social circles tended to overlap with political ones in the city and many of her friends moved in both. She met politicians and their friends at dinners, at the opera, at concerts. Not unexpectedly for such an attractive and eligible woman, Marion's name was linked with various men and for a short time she was escorted to concerts by the unlikely figure of politician Ted Heath, the Conservative leader and future Prime Minister. But maybe it was not as unlikely as it seemed. Marion and he shared a great love of music, Heath was a pianist, organist and orchestral conductor and they

The Stein family apartment in Vienna

The young Erwin Stein

Marion, a child in 1930's Vienna

Erwin Stein with friends, composers Anton
Webern and Arnold Schoenberg 1920s

Marion starting her career as a concert pianist

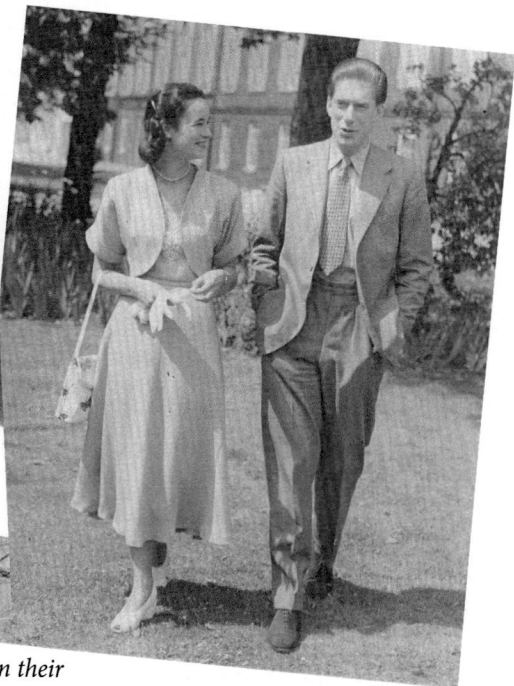

Marion and George on their
engagement day, 19 July 1949

Harewood House, West Yorkshire

The Wedding of the Year,
10 November 1949

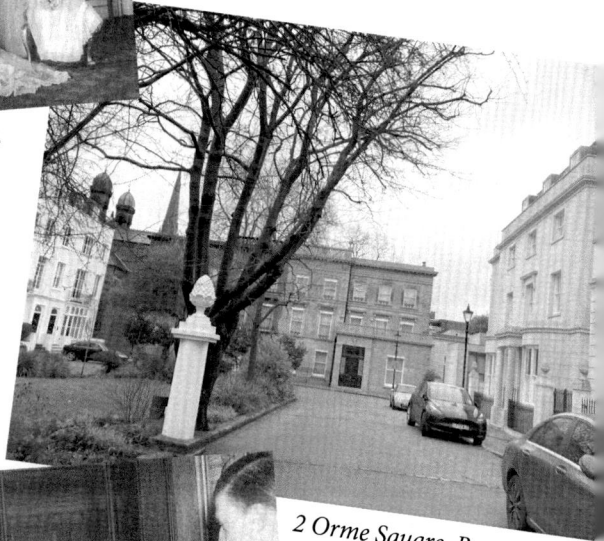

2 Orme Square, Bayswater.
Marion's London home

Visit to the opera at the Stoll Theatre, London 1952. Marion
and George with George's brother Gerald and his wife Angela

George and Marion concentrate on a run-through of Gloriana, Benjamin Britten's opera to celebrate the coronation of Elizabeth II

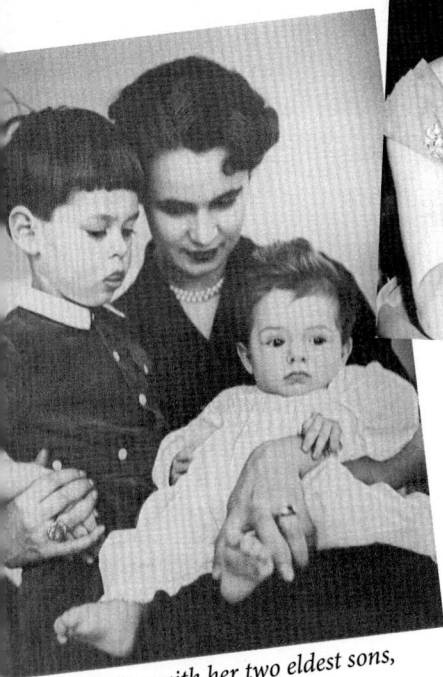

Marion with opera singer Maria Callas

Marion with her two eldest sons, David and baby James, 1953

In costume for the annual
Opera Ball at Covent Garden

Sightseeing in Moscow, 1963.
Peter Pears, Galina Rostropovich,
Benjamin Britten, Mstislav
Rostropovich and Marion

Marion and George om their first
trip to India, 1958

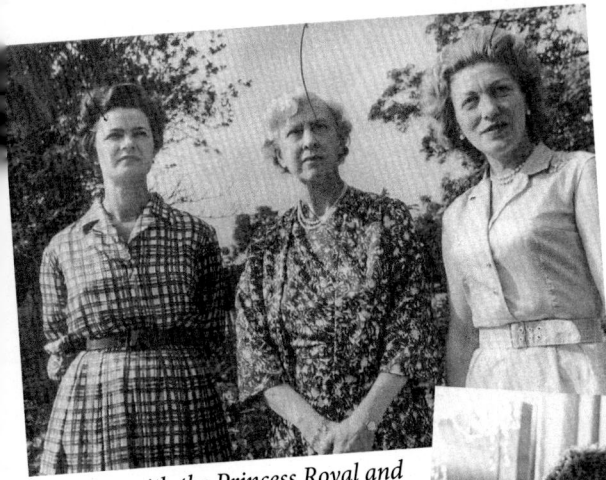
Marion with the Princess Royal and Angela Lascelles, 1964

Marion, Chair of the Friends of Covent Garden, speaking to members, May 1964

The first Leeds Piano Competition. Marion with the winner, Michael Roll, and founder Fanny Waterman

Curlews. Marion's seaside home at Thorpeness, Suffolk

Erwin Stein, Marion's father

Sophie Stein, Marion's mother

Marion and Jeremy Thorpe with
Jeremy's young son, Rupert

*A Musical Evening
to mark the Wedding of
Mr. and Mrs. Jeremy Thorpe*

PROGRAMME OF MUSIC

Robert Tear — John Constable (Piano)
 Four British Folk Songs: Arranged by Benjamin Britten
  The Plough Boy
  Sweet Polly Oliver
  O Waly, Waly
  Come you not from Newcastle

Yehudi and Hepzibah Menuhin
 Beethoven : Sonata for Violin and Piano in F Major
  " The Spring "
  Allegro; Adagio molto espressivo;
  Scherzo; Rondo

Janet Baker — John Constable (Piano)
 Schubert : Blumenlied
  An die untergehende Sonne
 Handel : Oh had I Jubal's Lyre

James Bowman, Peter Pears, John Shirley-Quirk
  Stuart Bedford (Piano)
 Benjamin Britten: Canticle IV " Journey of the Magi "
 Poem by T. S. Eliot

Clifford Curzon and Murray Perahia
 Mozart : Sonata for two pianos in D Major, K448
  Allegro con spirito; Andante; Allegro molto

ROYAL OPERA HOUSE SUNDAY,
COVENT GARDEN 22nd JULY, 1973

Musical Evening Programme, July
1973, to mark the wedding of Marion
and Jeremy Thorpe

Marion and Jeremy Thorpe with Rupert, late 1970s

Friends staying at Curlews for the Aldeburgh Festival 1976

Peter Pears, Marion and friends at Snape Maltings, 1985

Marion and Jeremy Thorpe 1994

had many friends in common, including Yehudi Menhuin and Clifford Curzon. The pianist Maura Lympany was a very close friend of Heath too and mutual friends even thought that they might marry. It was probably Maura who introduced Marion to Heath and although the two were never seen as a pair and the relationship was most definitely platonic, they enjoyed concert-going together. But it was to a politician of a different hue that Moura Lympany introduced her to on the evening of Monday, 17 January 1972. This was the dashingly attractive, recently widowed leader of the Liberal Party and amateur violinist, Jeremy Thorpe.

Moura knew Jeremy well, and he often escorted her to musical events. She had played at the concert at Barnstaple celebrating the dedication of the memorial to his wife Caroline. But on this cold January evening, she and Jeremy were in London at a recital given by her friend, the violinist Nathan Milstein. Marion had arranged a dinner party at Orme Square for Milstein after the recital and Madame Milstein requested that Moura and her escort be invited despite Marion not knowing Moura well and Thorpe not at all. According to Moura, just before the dinner, she had told Jeremy that although quite recently a widower, he should marry again, and that Marion would be ideal. He replied that he would not consider such a thing, but by the end of the evening, as he helped Marion pour coffee, he became more interested in his attractive host. "Moura, I think you're psychic," he later told his friend.

The Eton and Trinity College educated Thorpe had taken over the role of leader of his party from Jo Grimond in 1967, the same year that Marion was divorced from

Lord Harewood. He was considered a natural politician, Ted Heath referred to him as "a consummate leader of the Liberals, who certainly held his small party together. His Oxford Union experience stood him in good stead as a debater and despite his party's limited strength, he could be a commanding speaker in the House of Commons."[76] A lawyer by profession and particularly interested in human rights, he occasionally appeared in human rights cases without taking a fee. He represented twelve anti-apartheid demonstrators who had been arrested for protesting outside South Africa House and was known as an international humanitarian. The MP for North Devon since 1959, he had a large personal following there. Over the years he had charmed his constituents by his flamboyant personality and his extraordinary ability to remember not only the names of people he met, but also their concerns. He was called 'The King of Devon' and he adored being the centre of attention there. He visited Barnstaple often and his speeches were reported in the North Devon Journal newspaper as though the weighty offerings of a great statesman.[77]

"He had a style of his own: brown Trilby hat, waistcoat and gold watch-chain, and driving around in a big black Humber. With his powers of mimicry he could respond to hecklers in brilliant imitations of their own voice. He could mock people and win their vote.... His astonishing memory for faces and names enabled him to boom loud greetings to people in the streets and markets, to their lasting delight and the envy of their friends.

An entire generation of ladies took him to their hearts; he was mothered to distraction and I have come across several men now in their late forties and fifties named Jeremy in his honour."[78]

Thorpe was amusingly theatrical and aware of his smart and attractive looks. He was rather vain and how he came across to the public was important to him. In July 1967, just after he had become leader of his party, his wax effigy was unveiled at Madame Tussauds in London. The Daily Mail of 20 July reports his visit to see it. "My goodness," he exclaimed, "It looks like I have some terrible disease. I look quite death-like." When the hapless director of the museum suggested that in a different light it might look better, Jeremy argued that his predecessor Joe Grimond's waxwork looked fine in the same light. "If a dog happened to bite me," he continued, "I think the dog would be the one to get blood poisoning."

Although not everyone liked his flamboyant style, he had some very loyal people round him who were unofficial advisers. There were also personal friends with whom he could discuss issues outside of politics. One of these was his old school and Oxford friend David Holmes, merchant banker and deputy treasurer to the Liberal Party who had helped him with fundraising. Holmes was bisexual and understood Jeremy well. Much later however, his friendship would prove to be a well-meant though disastrous one. Equally close to Jeremy was German-born banker Robin Salinger, definitely heterosexual, who had married the young Iona Jones, Secretary to the Liberal Peers. After Jeremy's second marriage, the two couples became friends and Iona was close to Marion for the rest of her life.

Just a year after he became leader of the Liberal Party, Jeremy married the lively and popular thirty-year old

Caroline Allpass, after competing for her to some extent with his close friend. the bi-sexual David Holmes. Holmes happily supported his friend Jeremy's marriage and was, indeed, his best man at the wedding. Other friends and colleagues though, had doubts about Thorpe's marriage to Caroline. He was considered by them to be inexperienced heterosexually, unlike his potential wife, although he enjoyed the society of women and was considered a considerate and gallant companion. Views expressed in Liberal colleagues' diaries later, but not voiced openly at the time, were that he was marrying her for the wrong reasons – to increase his popularity with voters and possibly divert attention from rumours of his homosexuality – and they wondered what sort of husband he would prove to be.

"…. it is only the worse for poor Caroline Allpass who, it appears, is going to marry Jeremy …. She is rather a splendid girl all round and he is very lucky to have got someone like her. On the other hand, I can't help but feel she is extremely unlucky to have got him, since what he really wants is a wife for public consumption.[79]

There is no doubt that Thorpe was then an active homosexual, like many others at that time in politics. Although consensual, private acts between men over 21 had become lawful in 1967, to 'come out', intentionally or unintentionally would still have been the end of a political career. There were rumours about him and others but such rumours were well supressed and kept within the walls of the Commons. Only known to his closest friends, Thorpe was still indulging in homosexual encounters whilst engaged to Caroline. These were extremely risky to his reputation. Despite the changes in the law, public opinion about such sexual preferences in their representatives was still hostile. Caroline had many homosexual friends and had been told by Holmes that Jeremy was gay, or, like him, bisexual, so his previous sexual activity was unlikely to bother her, as long as she believed that it was in the past. Whether she did believe that this was the case was a cause for speculation at the time, but there are no reliable facts to support a belief either way. By all accounts Thorpe loved Caroline greatly and was delighted to be the father of a baby son, Rupert, born in 1969.

Just two years after his marriage, in June 1970, there was a general election. Thorpe's party did badly, despite a hectic month of electioneering with which Caroline had helped. She had had to perform the social duties of a political wife, look after the house and a small child when Jeremy was absent and cope with the presence of her overbearing mother-in-law, Ursula. She was understandably tired. On Monday 29 June she and Jeremy had to return to London from their cottage in Devon and it was decided that as there was still some packing to be done, Jeremy would take Rupert and his nurse by train to London and Caroline would drive there later with the luggage.

Later that afternoon, Iona Salinger, the young wife of Thorpe's great friend and financial adviser Robin, took a call in the party office. The news was devastating and not something she was prepared to tell Jeremy herself. After a witty speech in the House of Commons to congratulate the Speaker, Dr Horace King on his re-election, Thorpe went to his office with two colleagues to discuss the prospects for the party. There was a sudden interruption. The Superintendent of Police asked him to step out for a private word. Minutes later he collapsed into a chair ashen-faced and told his colleagues that Caroline had been in an accident. Unaccountably she had veered across the road near Basingstoke into oncoming traffic and struck a lorry and a car. She was dead.

Thorpe mourned 'theatrically' although genuinely for eighteen months. He filled the flat in London and the cottage in Devon with mementoes of Caroline, talked about her with everyone he met and created, probably for himself as much as for others, the memory of an ideal marriage. He organised an impressive memorial service before a packed congregation at St Margaret's, Westminster with the hymns sung at their wedding only two years before. He planned a shrine, which he referred to as his 'Taj Mahal' for the summit of Codden Hill near his home in North Devon, a hill he had climbed with Caroline. Although his grief was genuinely great, many thought his obsession with death and its rituals obsessive. But help was at hand in the form of two good friends. David Holmes attended to everything when Jeremy was in a state of shock and organised a private funeral. Caroline's childhood friend, Viv, came to live with him and look after Rupert. This kind but platonic relationship, as well as his great affection for his baby son, helped him though the next three years.

However, Jeremy was not the sort of man to bear his troubles quietly and privately. "Although Jeremy let the world know that he was devastated by his wife's death, he had little intention of withdrawing from public life. –

Indeed, his status as a public figure was consolation to him, and he played to perfection the part of a statesman bearing up in the face of personal tragedy." [80]

The tall obelisk on Codden Hill behind Thorpe's cottage, a memorial to Caroline, was finished in December 1971. Designing the memorial engaged his time end energy after the funeral, and seemed to act cathartically. Once it was completed, he was able to move on with his life. Although for many years he insisted in dragging new visitors to the cottage up the hill to see the memorial, he was able to resume leadership duties for his party and also to be seen more often in his social and musical circles.

The meeting at Orme Square of Marion and Jeremy led to a courtship of a year. They shared a love of music and were both musicians, she had been a concert pianist and he was a competent, albeit theatrical, amateur violinist. Her Jewish heritage was also attractive to Thorpe who was a committed friend to Israel throughout his political career Although "Marion doubtless preferred playing the piano to baking challah…she was fiercely proud of her Jewish heritage and Thorpe often referred to it".[81] But even more attractive to Marion was that he was different from her previous relationships and exciting. By the time Jeremy proposed at the Ritz on the 15 February 1973, a year after their meeting, they were still comparative strangers. They were both busy people and did not get to know each other very well before they married; much of their time together was with others, at operas, concerts and dinners. She had not met his formidable mother Ursula and he had not met her sons. Her life in Suffolk and his in Devon were still then unknown to the other. Whether by then she had heard the rumours of his homosexual past is not clear. Even many close colleagues in parliament claimed not to have known. Some were aware but chose to protect his reputation as he was the Liberal party's bright hope for the success of their party all through the 1960s and early 1970s. Any rumours about him remained rumours at that time. Unlike today, when members of Parliament come from a range of backgrounds and many are gay or gender fluid, for him to have come out in the 1970s would have been the death knell for his parliamentary career. Jeremy's sexual preferences were an open secret however in his constituency of North Devon where they were regarded as another of his many eccentricities. He often took male London friends there as political helpers. Just occasionally the open nature of such relationships was too much for his party. Michael Bloch in his biography of Jeremy Thorpe, quotes a situation when, at the annual Liberal Garden part at Lanhydrock in Cornwall in 1960, Jeremy, standing in for his friend Peter Bessel, the local MP, arrived with a 'handsome' youth who obviously had no interest in politics. Peter Bessell's wife Pauline, took exception and told Jeremy "Your relationship with that young man is obvious, please send him away."[82]

Bloch, a barrister and a writer, studied the homosexual backgrounds of 20th Century politicians including Thorpe. He writes,

> "It would be unfair to say he married purely for career reasons, for he enjoyed the company of women and his wives rescued him from the emotional tyranny of his mother. But his nature was fundamentally homosexual.... As Liberal leader

he kept a friend in his entourage who discreetly procured male partners; but there were moments of madness when he cruised the streets and haunted gay clubs... Thorpe clearly enjoyed the dangers inherent in these encounters, and on the whole handled them well."[83]

Most of these discreet male partners were just that. Many were prominent in their own communities, such as a Devon farmer, or they worked in sensitive roles, a policeman at the House of Commons. With those men he could feel safe. They too had much to lose from any publicity. It would have been likely that as time went by and the public began to accept the different sexual orientations of their representatives, any question of Jeremy's past homosexuality would cease to be important. They would also accept Thorpe for what he became, a happily married man. Unfortunately, however, Jeremy was unlucky. Instead of going away, questions about his sexuality continued to haunt him and would affect the whole trajectory of his future life. And that of Marion.

One of his early relationships, with a man called Norman Joliffe, (later calling himself Scott), surfaced to torment him. Scott felt aggrieved about his perceived treatment by Thorpe and became a thorn in the politician's side for well over a decade. Despite mostly successful attempts by friends and his party to protect his reputation by ways that pacified Scott and kept him away from Jeremy, there were periods when he felt particularly vulnerable, times when Norman Scott would emerge yet again demanding that everyone knew about his relationship with the famous

Liberal politician. It was the subsequent attempts to remove this threat, attempts that ultimately failed, that would eventually lead to his political and personal downfall.

It is thought that Jeremy did tell Marion in general terms about the trouble with a man who was pursuing him with claims of a previous gay relationship. But Jeremy was very persuasive. It is most likely that he convinced her it was the ravings of a sad, psychologically disturbed person, that there was no truth in his claims and that it was not important.

Marion was not naïve and had spent her teenage years living with Britten and Pears. They had a semi-public relationship and of course she knew both intimately. Like his first wife, it is unlikely she would have worried too much about Thorpe's previous homosexual activities, and like Caroline, would accept them if they remained in the past. But this was a time when such matters were not talked about publicly and she may have chosen to ignore any rumours. Not long after his marriage, it is reported, he discussed his recent marriage and his love life with his close friend Pater Bessell. Thorpe told him how happy he was with Marion, how she shared his enthusiasm for music and that she had bonded with his small son. But he admitted he still had occasional homosexual flings.

"Does Marion have any inkling?" Bessell asked.

"Certainly not," said Thorpe, and that was exactly how he intended to keep it.[84]

He told Bessell that he had raised the subject of homosexuality in a vague sort of way with Marion and received an unexpectedly extreme negative response; she had been shocked and disgusted. This seems strange. She had many gay friends. Perhaps the relationship she knew best, that of Britten and Pears was a more discreet, prim one than those that Jeremy was talking about. Perhaps her reaction was a personal one, intended to warn her husband off. She cannot have failed to be aware of some rumours about his past. Or perhaps the subject was not thought to be one that people discussed between men and women. At dinner on New Year's Eve 1971, Britten and a friend Graham Johnson had fiercely argued about the merits of the opera Rosenkavalier. Britten exploded, saying that he hated the piece, without more explanation. But the morning after, he apologised to a baffled Johnson, saying that what he loathed about the opera was its covert lesbianism, a subject he said he could not possibly have talked about in front of a woman. Marion had also been his dinner guest!

TWELVE

New Marriage

M arion and Jeremy kept the news of their engagement from all but close family. Her sons were surprised; "it came from left-field," but they were supportive. They had their own opinions about this new member of the family but could see that Jeremy made their mother happy and accepted her choice. Somehow, however, *The People* newspaper got wind of the story. Thorpe's press adviser rang him in Devon to warn him that the newspaper would run it on their front page on the 25 February 1973. Jeremy quickly broke the news to his constituency and returned to London the following morning to give a press conference with Marion at his home in Ashley Gardens. It was reported that Jeremy was in a lively, boyish mood, that Marion although unaccustomed to press conferences seemed sweet and natural, and that both he and Marion seemed delighted in each other. After that it seemed pointless to wait and the couple were married in a very secret wedding at Paddington Registry Office on the 14 March. Jeremy's good friend, banker Robin Salinger and Marion's eldest son David acted as their witnesses. It was a low-key affair, Marion wore a navy hat and coat, Jeremy his father's morning dress. Holy Communion from the Dean and a blessing from the Archbishop at Westminster Abbey followed before a luncheon party for forty. Marion's other sons James and Jeremy were there, and Marion's small new step-son, Rupert. Britten, despite being unwell with a heart complaint, would not miss the wedding of his close friend and came with Peter Pears. It was kept secret so successfully that the press did not get wind of the marriage until the couple were on their way to their first honeymoon, a few days in the South of France.

This first honeymoon was a short one due to Jeremy not wanting to be away from London for long. There seemed to be a Liberal revival and Thorpe's presence in Parliament as the party leader was needed. Two weeks in the Bahamas and the United States in Parliament's Easter recess was a second honeymoon. Marion had been to many places but never to the USA. Marion and Jeremy stayed some of the time there with Jack Hayward, a rich and valued supporter, who despite not being politically aligned with the Liberal party, liked Jeremy and saw in him a future prime minister. Not one to miss the chance of financial gain, Jeremy mixed business with pleasure and discussed with Jack the possibility of finding a buyer for Jack's business interests in the Bahamas. He saw the possibility of a large commission. Sometime later, he would have to cope with the consequences of his rather dubious efforts to make a profit from his friend.

Between the two honeymoons, the new Mrs Thorpe and her husband attended the wedding of her second son, nineteen-year-old James. James's band, road crew and their families lived together as a commune in an old thatched farm house in Sotherton in Suffolk. Marion had had so many twists and turns in her life so far that she was a pragmatist and took life as it came. Unlike how many other mothers would react against the plans of teenage sons who wanted to live a life completely different from that of their parents, she took it in her stride. supporting her second son's new and interesting life. She visited him in the commune and took her friends to visit, including the American actor Irene Worth, then playing a variety of classical roles in the London theatre. James married his American girlfriend, Frederica Duhrssen in April 1973, just a couple of months after Marion's own wedding. They had talked of a double wedding but in the event, the older couple married in London and the younger pair in Wortham, Suffolk. Frederica, the bride wore the lace dress worn by the Princess Royal at her wedding, the groom a sheepskin jacket and jeans. Specially composed songs in honour of the marriage were sung by the rock group to which James belonged. Jeremy, James' younger brother was a band member too, playing percussion. Both Marion and George, James's parents, attended the wedding with their new spouses. They were happy in their new lives and were able to see each other without apparent rancour at such important family occasions. But it was Marion who really supported James; she became a familiar figure at band concerts. "She came to the house, to gigs. Everyone got to know her," said James, "She was the family."

When Marion and Jeremy returned to London from America in May, Thorpe gave up his flat in Ashley Gardens just behind Westminster Cathedral and moved into Marion's large house in Orme Square with four-year old Rupert.

Being a mother of a young child came naturally to Marion. She enjoyed having a small boy in the family again, and helped Rupert to adjust to the changes of mothering in his life so far. He remembers being taken to the house in Orme Square when he was very small and playing hide and seek round the big sofas in the music room. A short time later he realised that this was to be his new home and he was taken up to the top of the house and shown his bedroom. There were two or three single beds there and always lots of people around, often hippies he remembered. Marion enjoyed the company of young people and encouraged their music-making although it was not really her taste. A friend of one of the boys, a member of James's band, the Global Village Trucking Company, remembers Marion as always having time for "a band of scruffy dropouts (us!) who she allowed to invade her exclusive residence." "She was 'lovely and kind to us," said another friend of Marion's sons. "as we rampaged throughout her home at all hours! I don't remember her once complaining." [85] Then it seemed to Rupert that suddenly the older boys moved out to pursue their own lives and careers and there were just the three of them, Jeremy, Marion and Rupert. Although the marriage seemed strange at first to his step-brothers and to many others, to him it seemed normal and that they made a very happy family. Jeremy and Marion were very different and they spent their time doing different things. Jeremy was often away with his various business and political projects. Marion had her own life in London, involved with her many musical interests. As Rupert grew up, he could always talk to Marion about things that concerned him and she was always knowledgeable and helpful although never pushed him to accept her opinion. Although affectionate, she was not too demonstrative and gave him space to decide things for himself. He was close to Lilia, who helped in the house and was an indispensable part of the household for many years She had fled Angola via Portugal and was probably not even the sixteen she claimed when she arrived. Rupert considers that she too was a 'mother' for him. The big house became his base and he went to the same school that Marion's other sons had attended when young, Hall School in Belsize Park.

The house itself "was an ideal house for a married statesman with a sense of the theatrical."[86] There were enough rooms to hold large receptions and dinners and to accommodate half a dozen guests. It had a first-floor balcony, ideal for a successful politician to speak to his public. It also had a rear entrance which allowed some privacy, a fact that the couple would appreciate in years to come. Marion still had Curlews, her house by the sea for some time and continued to spend time in Suffolk with friends, Britten and Pears. However, the cottage in Jeremy's North Devon constituency at Cobbaton a few miles from Barnstaple in Devon, a house that Jeremy had bought with his first wife Caroline, became their second home.

Higher Chuggaton in Devon is a listed cottage dating from about 1630 with a large garden which over many years grew into a beautiful oasis for Jeremy in particular. When Marion moved in, she and Jeremy planted bulbs that they had been given as a wedding present and each spring

Home Hill burst into a sea of daffodils. Marion accepted with good grace the mementoes to Caroline that were all over the cottage and the presence of the memorial on the nearby Codden Hill, which she too had been taken to see.

Caroline's outgoing personality had made her easily absorbed into the Devon community whereas Marion's outwardly reserved nature was very different. It took a little time for her to be accepted, but very soon she was seen as a valuable asset to the local Liberals. Her time as a Countess, when she regularly spoke at local events, served her well now. From being a minor member of the Royal family, she now had to adapt to the role of a politician's wife. Thorpe showed himself particularly attentive to Marion and they made a popular team when out canvassing for the Liberal party. To the surprise of some of his constituents who had expected the ex-Lady Harewood to need many servants, Marion adapted well to housekeeping at the cottage, although according to her family she was not a good cook and she did have people to help in the house. Much, much later, a reference in a television play to her cooking cod in parsley sauce to cheer up her husband caused much hilarity in the family. When in Devon, said her granddaughter Sophie, they often had Marks and Spencer ready-meals that did not need any cooking skills. Jeremy continued to enjoy developing the garden there. It was a good marriage; a love match, certainly one of mutual intrigue, and it remained so for many years. Despite Jeremy having been a young radical who reportedly regarded hereditary peerage as a medieval farce, he did love the romance of titles and he was fascinated by Marion's royal connections. Later he would pursue, unsuccessfully, the claim that he was heir to the barony of Thorpe. Marion liked his strong character and considered him, by all accounts, a rising political star. They found many more things in each other to admire. Jeremy cared about many causes, for example anti-apartheid in South Africa which she too supported. Thorpe told friends that they were bound together by shared suffering, having both been 'through the fiery furnace' owing to the traumatic loss (under different circumstances) of partners on who they had depended.[87] Her natural reserve was a foil for his natural enthusiasm.

Marion was very intelligent and enjoyed her new involvement in politics. Previously apolitical, she now robustly supported and defended the Liberal cause. Becoming more confident when dealing with the public as a politician's wife, she found it easier as time went on to get close to Jeremy's potential voters. She was naturally very open, affectionate, and funny although this had been masked by the apparent reserve required of her in her role as a countess. She was excited about her new role, the buzz of electioneering, the social whirl, and the promise of her husband's even more successful future in politics. She found her husband entertaining, unpredictable and exhilarating. Jeremy had a ribald sense of humour and a fund of stories. She and Thorpe laughed a lot together, and Marion missed him when he was away. The family recount how she loved to laugh and to tell jokes although was hopeless at telling them. She would confuse the order, forget the punchline, or be so amused herself that she would collapse into giggles before finishing.

Perhaps having had both a strong parent in Sophie and a mother-in-law Princess Mary, she was able to establish a good relationship with Jeremy's mother, the overbearing Ursula, who thought her son could do no wrong and was intensely ambitious for him. There were a lot of things that Ursula did not know about her son and Marion of her husband and the future would reveal some things both found extremely disconcerting. But this element of intrigue was a key part of Thorpe's make-up and not unattractive to his wife. And above all she was a pragmatist. She would cope with whatever came her way.

On 22 July 1973, four months after their wedding, they celebrated with a party at Covent Garden. Over a thousand guests, from all walks of life; the family, from politics, from music, from James's commune, were all treated to a champagne reception in the crush bar followed by a 'Musical Evening to mark the Wedding of Mr. and Mrs. Jeremy Thorpe' given by many of the musical elite of the day. Most were friends of Marion who she had met during her marriage to George. They were happy to support her at the start of this new stage in her life, in her new marriage to Jeremy Thorpe. Janet Baker sang Schubert, Yehudi and Hepzibah Menuhin played Beethoven and Clifford Curzon and Murray Perahia performed a Mozart sonata for two pianos. Britten, although too ill to attend the party, chose an arrangement of British folk songs sung by Robert Tear and accompanied by John Constable as his contribution. James Bowman, Peter Pears and John Shirley-Quirk, accompanied by Stuart Bedford sang Britten's Canticle IV, Journey of the Magi. Some radical Liberals thought the party elitist and some old Etonians saw it as rather showy. When he heard of these comments, Jeremy exploded with rage. "One has to bloody well lead one's own life…. It's my wedding. If one cannot have a reception such as one wants, then to hell with them. One has made enough sacrifices in one's personal life. They can find another leader."[88]

The next year was a successful one both for the couple personally and for the Liberals. In July 1973, just after the wedding party, the Liberals won two constituencies from the Tories in one day, at that time, an historical feat, only to be equalled in 2022. Two constituencies had become vacant: Ely after the death of Conservative MP Harry Legge-Burke, and Ripon whose Tory MP Sir Malcolm Stoddart-Scott had also recently died. Marion and Jeremy campaigned vigorously in the Isle of Ely constituency close to Aldeburgh where Marion was based when not in London. Clement Freud, a friend of Jeremy's became the new MP there. Leeds bookseller David Austick was successful too and won the seat in Ripon. The Liberals were back into double figures of MPs. To celebrate, Marion and Jeremy held a champagne party at a Westminster pub and then presided at a reception for the new MPs at the National Liberal Club. Marion had a great gift for adapting herself to new situations. By the end of her first year of marriage to Jeremy she was pitched into intensive campaigning, principally by helicopter for the general election which was scheduled for February 1974. The following months saw some ups and downs in the fortunes of both Jeremy and the Party and the year 1973 did not end well for him. The secondary banking firm of London and County Securities, of which he had been a director collapsed amid rumours of mismanagement and fraud. He managed to avoid too much censure by promising to support shareholders.

However, 1974 started hopefully. The threat from

Norman Josiffe (now calling himself Scott) seemed to have died down and Jeremy's political ambitions seemed about to be realised. Marion's first grandchild Sophie, a daughter for her son James and his wife, had arrived in October 1973. At the time James and his wife Frederica were staying in Suffolk and their daughter Sophie was born at Curlews, Marion's house near Aldeburgh, in a room that later became Rupert's. Jeremy was delighted that he was now a grandfather, albeit step, as well as a father. Curlews too was the temporary base for Mstislav Rostropovich (Slava) the famous cellist and a critic of Soviet politicians. A close friend of Benjamin Britten, who was quite ill by then, and of Marion, he was welcomed to Aldeburgh when he left the Soviet Union for a self-imposed exile. As ever, Marion opened her home and heart to any friend who needed somewhere to live and as Britten could not entertain Slava at the Red House, the cellist stayed at Curlews. Rupert tells the story of how Slava was staying in the bedroom next to his and the two of them used to play chess and checkers together. Seeing the cello in its case, the young boy asked what it was. Told it was a cello and Slava's 'baby', Rupert asked Slava to play it. When the cellist said he would not as he was too sad, Rupert persuaded him to take out the cello and play. Rupert is proud that he most likely heard the very first performance of the great cellist after he left his home country.

The next couple of years were sometimes happy but also sometimes fraught times for Jeremy. The couple's relationship was good and they were beginning to learn more about each other. Marion however would probably never know the complications of the life that her husband led, nor would be aware of how he was regarded by many of his contemporaries. His was a character which generated polarised views. Marion was attracted by his ebullient personality, his wit, his zest for life and she was impressed at how so many of his constituents warmed to his friendly and outgoing personality. Other views of him by opponents were less favourable: opportunist, showman, sinister and exhibitionist were just some of the epithets attached to his name by those who disliked him.

Marion continued to be busy with her musical activities. On New Year's Eve 1973 she was the guest on BBC Radio 4's *Desert Island Discs*, a recognition of her role in the musical life of the country. Interestingly she was interviewed not as Mrs Jeremy Thorpe but as musician, Marion Stein. Perhaps when she was booked for the programme she was not yet married. But I like to think she was firmly stating that she was not an ex-countess or a political wife, but was above all, a musician in her own right. Sadly, a recording of the programme no longer exists but a list of her choices does. It reflects musical influences at different times in her life. Her favourite choice was the final track of Bach's *St Matthew Passion*. She also requested Mozart's *Piano Concerto number 20*, Verdi's *Falstaff* and Beethoven's *Cello Sonata No. 2*. Her favourite composer was Mahler and she chose *Der Abschied* from *Das Lied von der Erde*. She must have spoken to the interviewer about her closeness to Benjamin Britten and Peter Pears and the listeners then heard their version of Schubert's *Frulingstraum* from *Wintereisse* and Britten's *Spring Symphony*. Her interest in modern music fostered by her father Erwin showed in 'Onkel' Alban's (Berg's) *Three fragments of Wozzeck*, which must have brought back memories, as it was after a performance of the opera in 1949 that her first husband had asked her to marry him. She chose Goethe's *Faust* as the only book to accompany her to the desert island, and as her one luxury, the score of Mozart's *The Magic Flute*, the first opera she had been allowed to see as a child, long ago in Vienna. Marion's musicianship was well known at the time and she also appeared as an occasional panellist on the long-running BBC radio quiz 'Face the Music'. A panel of three music-loving celebrities and an invited guest answered musical questions put to them by host Joseph Needham. During its most popular period, the weekly quiz had over four million listeners and it lasted for seventeen years.

In the early 1970s, Marion became concerned that her good friend Benjamin Britten was ailing and it seemed likely that soon he would no longer be able to accompany his partner Peter Pears in their recitals of Schubert, Schumann and Britten songs. She was still very much involved with the Leeds International Piano Competition and decided to introduce the winner of the 1972 competition, twenty-five-year-old pianist Murray Perahia, to Ben and Peter. In September, not long after his success in Leeds, Murray went with Marion to a recital at Snape Maltings, Britten's concert hall near Aldeburgh, and heard Pears sing. The three men met again at a concert at the Edinburgh Festival and Pears asked Perahia to play for him at the next Aldeburgh Festival. Britten approved but insisted on attending the final run-through; a nervous occasion for the young pianist. Murray continued to accompany Pears in some recitals until the older man retired.

Music was important but so also was her new role as

a political wife. In early 1974 the Liberals feared the rise of the Conservative vote but felt prepared for the general election in February. In the previous November, the Party had managed to win Berwick in a by-election - just - after a recount despite their expectation that they would romp home. Lord Lambton, the previous Conservative MP for Berwick had stood down after being photographed by the *News of the World* smoking cannabis with a call girl. Jeremy, in a radio interview at the time had played the moral card in supporting his own candidate.

> "If you are in public life, you are more vulnerable and must not put yourself in a position where you can be subject to blackmail or other pressures, peccadilloes which might be acceptable for a private citizen can become a great danger to security with a person in public life."

In retrospect this was rather rich coming from Jeremy Thorpe. Those words would come back to haunt him. Either he did not think such rules applied to him or he was confident that his own 'peccadilloes' were known only to those who would keep their mouths firmly shut.

In early 1974, Thorpe retreated to Devon with Marion and his assistants to defend his fragile majority. Always ready to use technology to his advantage he set up a closed-circuit television link between the Liberal Offices in Barnstaple and his London headquarters at the National Liberal Club. He sat serenely at an antiques desk and gave a long-distance press conference every morning whilst other politicians squabbled in London. Marion campaigned with her husband locally, much needed help as boundary changes meant that there were far more new constituents in the North Devon constituency, many of them unfamiliar with their candidate. Jeremy was in good form, interacting in a lively way with his constituents and journalists in Devon but he toned down his ebullience on the TV screen. Marion appeared alongside Jeremy in an amusing film about him, and Marion's devotion shown to her husband was apparent. She was becoming a great asset as a political wife. Jeremy retained his seat with an increased majority. The result gave rise to a hung Parliament in which Thorpe held a pivotal place, the Liberals having won a sizeable number of votes. There was a possibility that he would be given an active role in government, one which he sought. However, after much debate and discussion, with some of his MPs believing he was not consulting them, he finally refused to join the government of the Conservative Edward Heath as Home Secretary. When Heath's Conservative government began to fail, the Liberals scored a few by-election victories but the chance of him leading the Liberals as part of government had passed him by, at least for the foreseeable future. Although some Liberal supporters were disappointed that he had not struck a deal with Heath, he won the approval of the public, being seen as having sacrificed office for the good of his party, and his support as a leader increased. Both he and Marion spoke to friends. as though his time in government was not far off.

When the Heath government finally fell and another election was triggered, Jeremy once again set off on the campaign trail in Devon, Marion accompanying him. That summer he was embarrassed, or at least his party was, by the failure of one of his flamboyant attempts at publicity for the Liberals, a failure which was regarded as typical of his flagging leadership. He was the first politician to embrace the television age, having used it to excellent effect to boost his popularity in the February election that year. He had been the first to use a helicopter on the campaign trail. So, true to form, in the summer of 1974, and funded by his backer Jack Hayward, he chose the glamorous novelty of a hovercraft to tour the South West. The plan was that he would be accompanied by Marion and his aides and that local Liberal candidates would join at each port. It went well at first. Brass bands greeted the hovercraft when it landed and thousands of startled holidaymakers listened as Jeremy, in Edwardian seaside costume, addressed them from the deck with a loud-hailer. So far, so good. However, a freak wave damaged the hovercraft at Sidmouth, the patched-up vehicle suffered bad weather and engine trouble and could not land at some places as planned. The tour ended in disaster when, at one stop, he had just reached the point in his speech when he was praising the fine new invention of the hovercraft when he realised that his feet were getting wet. The hovercraft was sinking beneath him. The vehicle had to be abandoned as it had broken down conclusively. The press could not fail to be amused by the debacle and it was considered an embarrassment by the party. How Marion felt when she and her damp husband had to transfer ignominiously to a car for the rest of their tour, is unknown.

The second election of 1974, in October that year gave Labour under Harold Wilson a slender majority. Harold Wilson liked Jeremy despite their political differences. One day Wilson, on the way to make an election speech in Barnstaple, met Jeremy, also on the way to his North Devon constituency. Jeremy suggested that Wilson share his car. On a Devon country road, the car was stopped by a load of hay which had fallen off a lorry. The two men helped to re-load the hay. Wilson arrived in Barnstaple late for his appearance and sprinkled with hay.

Wilson sincerely believed that Jeremy was sometimes under threat because of his support for the anti-apartheid movement in South Africa. It was this mistaken supposition that would later contribute unintentionally to Thorpe's troubles.

Thorpe's Liberal party's performance at the election was disappointing. He also had to deal with other difficulties in his personal and public life. He was relieved that he had managed to convince his supporter Jack Hayward that it was a friend of his, Peter Bessell, and not he who had tried to defraud the financier over the sale of Bahamian assets. More upsetting, his sister had taken an overdose and died aged 48, a sadness and an embarrassment to him. His adored grandmother had died too, aged 101.

Thorpe was now in a weakened position as Liberal leader. He would need to fight for his political survival. Although he tried to protect Marion from his problems, especially unpleasant things from his past and those that did not reflect well on him, she must have seen how nervous he was. Although she did not know the details of the complicated story, her husband was increasingly aware of the presence in Devon of the man who he had tried to pass off as a madman; Norman Scott; the man who was telling his story about a homosexual relationship with Jeremy to anyone who would listen.

Around Easter 1975, Jeremy's attempts to keep Marion unaware of the story of Norman Scott failed. Scott had been beaten up and had a briefcase of papers stolen. He was frightened. Believing that Thorpe was behind what had happened and wanting his files back, he decided to confront Jeremy. Although both lived at times in Devon, they had not met for over ten years. In his old Morris 1100, recently bought with the proceeds of incriminating letters from Jeremy that he had recently sold, a hysterical Scott drove up to the cottage at Cobbaton. He managed to drive down the narrow lane and parked the car. Marion was in the cottage and six-year-old Rupert was playing in the garden. Scott knocked at the door. When Marion answered, he introduced himself and asked to speak to Jeremy. How he introduced himself and what he claimed to be his relationship with Thorpe is not recorded. But he was upset, even hysterical about what he thought were plots to silence him. And this was not just paranoia, plans were indeed afoot. One of Thorpe's best friends and supporters David Holmes, who was the assistant treasurer of the liberal Party later admitted to being behind the two incidents that had frightened Scott: a robbery in Barnstaple of his papers by two men claiming to be journalists, and the beating up of Scott a few weeks earlier as he left a pub. Marion showed no outward surprise at Scott's outburst but coolly said that she did not think her husband would see him. Scott got back in his car in tears, but in his panic, missed a gear change and slid into the garage doors. He had to ask Marion to help him. "Which she did in grim silence." [89]

Jeremy had failed to protect her from the unpleasantness of his problem with Norman Scott. From this point on

Marion would increasingly become aware of her husband's past. Not only Thorpe's political career but his marriage could be threatened. It was even mor imperative to remove the threat posed by Scott.

But reader, let us pause as Norman Scott drives erratically away from Marion, standing by the door of the cottage in Cobbaton, watching him leave. The tale of Scott and his claimed relationship with Jeremy Thorpe, needs to be told briefly and understood before Marion's story continues. She would be profoundly affected by what happened to her husband in the following years. By this time, action was already being planned by her husband's loyal allies to keep Norman Scott from ruining Thorpe's political and personal life. What role Jeremy played in this action and what he knew became core questions at the heart of what came next. The unfolding of the story and the repercussions of such actions would test Marion's loyalty to its utmost.

THIRTEEN

Scott and Thorpe

Jeremy Thorpe met Norman Josiffe (he only took the name Scott in 1967) in late 1960 or early 1961 at Kingham Stables, Chipping Norton, Oxfordshire. He was visiting a friend, the owner Norman Vater. Josiffe, having learned to ride when on probation for a minor offence of theft as a teenager, was working for Vater as a groom. Somewhat of a fantasist; he had severed all links with his family, changed his name to Lianche-Josiffe and hinted that he had aristocratic connections. Thorpe chatted to the groom and was sufficiently attracted to this good-looking young man that he casually suggested that if Josiffe ever needed help, he could contact him. A fateful mistake as it turned out. A short time later, Josiffe fell out with his employer, had a nervous breakdown and was under psychiatric care for some time. When, by late 1961 he was ready to go back to work, he needed his insurance card. As he had left Vater's with bad feelings, he did not want to contact the stable owner to retrieve it. So, remembering Jeremy Thorpe's offer of help, he went to see him at the House of Commons.

According to Josiffe, so began a homosexual relationship with Thorpe, the first occasion being that evening at the house of the MP's mother in Oxted. The younger man always insisted that Thorpe had introduced him to homosexual practices that night. Thorpe always denied that such an event ever took place and never wavered from his assertion. According to him, any relationship with Scott was based on providing support for one of his constituents. For several years however, Josiffe was helped by Thorpe who organised accommodation first in London and then in his Devon constituency, arranged a series of temporary jobs and promised to help Josiffe train in dressage. This could be viewed as generosity on the part of Thorpe to support a needy constituent. But a major problem was that he also wrote letters to Josiffe, many which were affectionate and compromising. Josiffe kept them all. In April 1962 the young man obtained a replacement insurance card which he said was then retained by Thorpe 'as his employer'. Thorpe denied any knowledge of this but the lost card became an ongoing source of grievance to Josiffe out of all proportion to any problem of replacing a card and was one reason for his simmering resentment of Thorpe.

The following years showed Josiffe in various states of mental health, talking to the police and anyone else who would listen about his affair with Thorpe. He showed his letters to the police as proof. At this stage, his story was not taken seriously by the authorities, Josiffe being seen as unreliable and hysteric. For a while he was quiet but by early 1965 on Scott's return to England from Switzerland the situation had become more stressful for Jeremy Thorpe.

His political career was on the rise and he could not afford his past to hinder his success.

Then working in Dublin, Josiffe pestered Thorpe about a missing suitcase of letters and his lost insurance card; responsibility for either was firmly rejected by the MP. But when Josiffe wrote a long letter to Thorpe's adoring mother Ursula, giving her graphic details of what he said was his affair with her son and blaming him for "this vice that lies latent in every man," Thorpe knew he needed help. He turned to another MP, Peter Bessell who was a great admirer and a personal friend. Bessell took it on himself to shield his friend from any publicity that would affect his chances of becoming the leader of the Liberal Party. He had gained Thorpe's confidence by claiming that he himself was bisexual. The two men had gone on to have a long discussion about their tendencies, Thorpe claiming to be 80% gay, Bessell lied and said he was 20% gay. The latter was totally heterosexual and led a very complicated life with his women partners. But on one thing they firmly agreed; if anyone ever found out about it, neither would ever be leader of the Party.

Over the next few years, Bessell's efforts kept Norman, now having changed his name to Scott, quiet. He took on himself the role of protector. With Thorpe's knowledge but careful not to implicate Jeremy, who was now the Liberal leader, Bessell responded to Scott's requests for help, accommodation or financial support. But in 1968, the problem of Scott re-emerged. The timing was particularly dangerous for Thorpe. He was struggling to establish himself as the new leader of the Party and was newly married to Caroline, his first wife. He did not want any trouble.

What happened next has been the subject of much discussion, covered in books about the 'Thorpe Affair' and easily available to interested readers. What Bessell with David Holmes, along with others planned to do about Scott and how much Jeremy knew about the plan was eventually to become the essence of a court case. There is no doubt that Thorpe wanted Scott's silence; he wanted the threat posed by the younger man to his personal and political futures removed. But what methods were discussed and agreed to for such riddance is still questioned fifty years on. It appears that waiting for the division bell one day in 1969, Jeremy and Bessell discussed 'killing' Scott. Jeremy liked to amuse friends with speculations, and a crowded corridor in the House of Commons seems a strange place to hatch serious plans. A short time later at a meeting of Thorpe, Holmes and Besssell, the three were said to have again discussed plans for ridding Thorpe of Scott. What 'ridding 'meant would be a basis for debate throughout future criminal investigations. According to Thorpe's two friends, they agreed to consider an alleged suggestion from Thorpe to kill Scott off, afraid of what actions Jeremy might take himself if they refused. Jeremy to his dying day maintained he never made such a suggestion. Whatever the truth of that meeting, a reprieve seemed to have been granted when Scott, unexpectedly got married and had a child, but within a couple of years Scott's marriage collapsed. Again, Thorpe was being blamed volubly by Scott for his woes and threatened with exposure.

In 1971, Scott moved to North Wales and befriended a widow, Gwen Parry-Jones. Scott was a fantasist, over time making up many different stories about his antecedents. He also had a talent for convincing new acquaintances that he was misunderstood and mistreated, and Mrs Parry-Jones was no exception. After listening to his story, she contacted the Liberal MP for nearby Montgomeryshire, Emlyn Hoosen, no friend of Thorpe. Hoosen suggested that Scott come to see him at the House of Commons, along with David Steel, the Liberals' chief whip. The two politicians were very concerned. Despite a confidential party enquiry to investigate Scott's claims, chaired by Lord Byers, the leader of the Liberals in the House of Lords, Thorpe once again managed to convince the inquiry that they should dismiss the allegations as those of a hysteric who was mentally ill. Unfortunately for Jeremy, this inflamed Scott's resentment rather than putting the matter to rest.

Scott pursued his vendetta: In March 1972, his friend Gwen Parry-Jones died and he used her inquest to denounce Thorpe once again for ruining his life and for driving his friend to her death by suicide. But no newspaper would publish his story. For the following couple of years, Scott was relatively subdued, living quietly in Devon and on tranquilizers. By that time, Thorpe was becoming more successful. He married Marion in early 1973 and she campaigned with him in the general election of February 1974 and helped his cause considerably. She was increasingly popular in his constituency. The Liberals did well and for a short time there was a possibility that the Liberals might work in coalition with the Conservatives. However, another election in October saw the Liberals lose votes and the Labour party under Harold Wilson form a minority labour Government.

Thorpe would have been well-aware that Scott was

once again active but Marion would have no idea of the new threat. She must have been aware of her husband's increased nervousness in 1974 although it was 1975 before she was confronted by Scott at the Devon cottage. Perhaps she assumed his agitation was concern about his political difficulties, but it is far more likely that it was the due to the recurring problem of Norman Scott. It would not go away. Scott had re-emerged from his quiescent period in January and had contacted Tim Keigwin, Thorpe's Conservative opponent in North Devon. The Conservative leadership advised Kiegwin not to use the material. Whether rumour of this reached Thorpe it is unknown, but someone probably alerted him. A more critical problem emerged later that year. Scott had told his story to his doctor, Ronald Gleadle, who was treating him for depression, and shown the doctor his collection of documents. Gleadle contacted Thorpe about the papers, and, strangely unprofessional for a professional medical man, offered them for sale. David Holmes, who had just taken over as Thorpe's protector after Bessell's move to California, agreed to buy them for £2,500, financed anonymously by Thorpe. These were burned at the home of Thorpe's solicitors. Hopefully, the threat of exposure had been averted. But then a discovery by builders of more incriminating papers and photographs in a briefcase hidden in an office formerly used by Bessell made the situation even worse. The situation was becoming like an improbably written crime novel. The builders took their find to the Sunday Mirror which, after keeping copies of the documents, passed the briefcase on to Thorpe.

Bessell, now in California, either in a real attempt to protect his friend, or to re-take his place in the drama, decided to take full responsibility for Scott's behaviour and not involve Jeremy. He rang Thorpe to tell him of this decision but it was Marion that replied. She was very cold and when asked if she could ask Jeremy to phone California, she replied "I could". And put down the phone. Marion, having as most people had, a confused picture of what was going on, and not being told the full story by Jeremy, had decided that Bessell was bad for Jeremy and that it was he who had broken the story to the papers. Despite feeling very sympathetic towards Thorpe, and appreciative for Jeremy's thanks for his support, Bessell was unhappy about Marion's treatment of him. "You know that I have done all I can to be helpful over many, many years... for these reasons I am mystified about Marion's attitude. She treated me like excrement on the 'phone and this is wholly unjustified."[90] Whether Marion's dislike for Bessell coloured Jeremy's opinion of his old friend or not, he would treat him in the future with hostility; treatment to which the previously patient and loyal Bessell would eventually react.

Exposure must have seemed very close to Thorpe. His political career, and probably his new marriage was threatened. Norman Scott was not going to keep quiet. It was at this time, according to Holmes, although always refuted by Jeremy, and never believed by Marion, that his friend again insisted that they should get rid of Scott. Whether Thorpe really wanted Scott dead or just frightened off was a key question, Holmes changing his mind more than once when questioned later. The quote often attributed to Henry II "Will no one rid me of this turbulent priest?" which was taken as an order by his followers and resulted in the death of Thomas Becket is commonly used now to express that a leader's wish may be interpreted, wrongly, as a command. There is little doubt that Jeremy wanted Scott out of his hair and that very loyal friends were willing to help. However, he was a showman and often used vivid and emotive language which could have been misinterpreted.

What happened next was worthy of the plot for a murder mystery. Holmes, obviously new to finding someone to silence Scott, involved a bizarre group of co-conspirators. He talked to John Le Mesurier, a carpet dealer, who put him in contact with George Deakin, a gambling machine manufacturer from Swansea, who, in turn found Andrew Newton, an airline pilot, who agreed to deal with Scott for £10,000. What precise message eventually reached Newton from Holmes via Le Mesurier and Deakin, and even possibly another link in the chain, would be vigorously debated in the future. Later evidence suggests that at this time Jack Hayward, totally innocently, provided £50,000 cash at the request of Thorpe, supposedly as a contribution to election expenses. Thorpe asked for two payments of £10,000 to be sent to a different bank account. This money was never accounted for.

After Scott's visit to the cottage at Easter 1975, Marion could not be kept in the dark about the problems that Norman Scott was posing for her husband although she was totally unaware of any plot that was being hatched. The arrival of Scott at his home seems to have been the last straw for Thorpe's delicate psychological state due to his fear of exposure. That summer he seemed to undergo some sort of breakdown. He stayed at the cottage in Devon for six weeks and Marion, now an experienced political wife, had to fulfil his engagements. He revived however in time for the Liberal Assembly at Scarborough in September and made a well-received speech that reasserted his hold on the party leadership. His changing moods in and out of both positiveness and abstraction may have been due to knowing that, at last, steps to rid him of Scott were going to be taken or perhaps they were the initial symptoms of a future illness.

In early October 1975, Newton met Holmes to receive the down payment on the fee of £10,000 for silencing Scott. Holmes for many years contended that the robbery and beating up of Scott as well as what came later, were always intended to frighten Scott off and no more. On the contrary, Mesurier in later interviews contended that he was asked to find a hit man to carry out a contract killing. Either there was a misunderstanding or one of them was lying. So many people were involved in the plan and stories were changed so often that it is difficult to ascertain the truth.

In late October, the farcical plan to silence Scott was put into action.

FOURTEEN

Revelations

The story now is well known. The hired gunman Andrew Newton, calling himself Peter Keene, approached Scott explaining that he had been hired to protect him from a Canadian hit man. This seemed plausible to Scott as he was in a heightened state of panic and paranoia after the attack and robbery and agreed to meet Newton at Coombe Martin a few days later. Luckily, a friend of Scott, suspicious of 'Keene' noted the number of his yellow Mazda hire car. Meeting up with Newton on 24 October 1975, Scott agreed to drive with Newton to Porlock and back, so that they could talk. Newton was not happy with having to take Scott's Great Dane Rinka in the Ford Escort he was now driving, but Scott insisted and so all three set off to Porlock. There, Newton feigned going off on 'business' while Scott waited with Rinka. By the time Newton returned to the car it was dark and there were few other cars travelling the road. At the top of Porlock Hill, Newton feigned tiredness, pulled into a deserted lay-by and Scott suggested that he take over the driving. As

Scott came round to the driver's side, Rinka jumped out too. Newton pointed the gun at Rinka and shot him dead and then turned the gun on Scott. The gun jammed, and after a few more unsuccessful attempts, Scott fled a short distance. Newton jumped into the car and sped off, leaving a distressed Scott to return to the side of his dead pet and flag down a passing motorist.

Thanks to the friend who had the number of the hired Mazda, Newton was quickly traced, and sent for trial. The news of Newton's arrest was relayed by Holmes to Jeremy, and for a short time Jeremy's speeches lacked his customary flair. Realising that he was not being implicated by Newton, his speeches improved. Marion suggested he dispensed with his scriptwriter and spoke off-the-cuff at his rallies and this seemed to help. Newton made no mention of any deal with Holmes at his trial, and in March 1976 was sent to prison for two years.

But a can of worms was opening. As early as December 1975, Private Eye's Auberon Waugh was beginning to highlight the connection of Jeremy Thorpe to Norman Scott. In his 'diary' that month he reported that "West Somerset is buzzing with rumours of a most unsavoury description following reports in the West Somerset Free Press about an incident which occurred recently on Exmoor. Mr Norman Scott of North Devon who claims to have been a great friend of Jeremy Thorpe, the liberal Statesman, was found by an AA patrolman weeping beside the body of Rinka, his Great Dane bitch, who had been shot in the head. .... My only hope is that sorrow over his friend's dog will not cause Mr Thorpe's premature retirement from public life." Over the next two years Private Eye did much to untangle or tangle, depending on what readers believed, the web connecting Thorpe to the supposed assassination attempt.

In January 1976, Scott appeared in the Magistrates court on a minor charge relating to social security and took the chance of informing the court of his grievances against Jeremy. As this was a court, there were no reporting restrictions and the story was widely reported. Other investigations began. The Daily Mail interviewed Peter Bessell in California who said that it was he who had been blackmailed by Scott but left Thorpe out of his story. Other newspapers published the fact that Holmes had bought Scott's papers from Dr Gleadle. David Steel, the Liberal Chief Whip discovered the £20,000 intended for the Party had gone to Holmes and was unaccounted for. It was a tangled web but, mixing my metaphors, the net was closing on Thorpe. On 14 March 1976 the Sunday Times, a paper reasonably friendly to him, published a detailed rebuttal by Jeremy 'The Lies of Norman Scott' on its front page. It was hoped by Marion and Jeremy that this would quieten the interest in the case.

The article did not help. Things got worse for Jeremy. Bessell, feeling unhappy and understandably resentful about how his erstwhile friend was treating him (Thorpe had written to Jack Hayward and referred to Bessell as 'that bastard Bessell') told the Daily Mail that he had lied to protect Thorpe. His loyalty for his friend was eroded but also, as ever keen on the limelight, he chose to speak to the press. He was also very aware about how people regarded his honesty. A statement from Scott in the witness box at Andrew Newton's trial "Mr Bessell, you will find, in the end, will tell the truth," resonated with him.

As almost a last-ditch attempt to salvage his reputation, Thorpe published two of his early letters to Scott in the Sunday Times, ones that referred to Scott as 'Bunnies,' expressing love for Scott and saying he was missed. It was an attempt to explain the letters as merely friendly and helpful to a constituent. It is thought that friends urged him to talk to Marion about the letters the night before their publication. She might have been shocked if she had read them without his explanation. How he explained them to her is not known, but there was no change in her outward expressions of support for her husband. In retrospect, however, allowing the letters to be published was a mistake. Although the article was supportive and quoted a speech from Harold Wilson saying that 'underground forces' were at work against the leader of the Liberal party, the 'Bunnies' letter amused the public and the Liberal Party was a laughing stock. That weekend, Marion and Jeremy left for their house in Suffolk, waiting for the Sunday papers. It does not take much imagination to think how Marion would be feeling about the situation her husband was in or what she would be thinking about 'Bunnies'. Perhaps she did not ask, preferring to keep her thoughts to herself. But she was incensed by the way that the press treated her husband. She had been familiar with press intrusion before. When she was a young woman engaged to a member of the royal family, she had been followed by photographers and journalists. But this was different. They were now hostile rather than friendly. And she needed to protect her husband if she could. That weekend the media were preoccupied with the story. Richard Wainwright, a fellow Liberal MP, interviewed on Radio Leeds, asked why, if Jeremy knew he had nothing to hide, he did not sue for libel. Maybe this suggestion was intended to help but Jeremy was not likely to sue. Most commentators now believed that Thorpe had not told the truth and the letters made him and the Liberals seem ridiculous. That Sunday afternoon Jeremy and Marion went over to Ely to see their good friend Clement Freud. Gently, Freud told Jeremy that he should resign. His advice was as a friend who feared that Jeremy, constantly harried by the press, was heading for a breakdown. Marion would have been able to tell Clement about how Jeremy was reacting, almost at the end of his tether. The following day Jeremy Thorpe wrote to the Liberal Chief Whip David Steel, his early protégé and the man who would succeed him, and resigned as leader of the Liberal Party.

How did Marion feel about what was happening to her? She was, as those who knew her say, extremely stoical. She was one of a breed of people of her generation who were brought up to cope with whatever life threw at them and to be, if necessary, self-sacrificing. She had already coped with major unforeseen and upsetting things in her life. Could she talk to anyone about how she was feeling and what she should do? This would not be likely. Both her parents were dead and her good friend Ben Britten, who would have been someone who understood the complexities of her marital situation, was very ill. She could get very angry, she was a passionate woman, but would not show it outside her family and very close friends however she felt inside. Only very occasionally, and as a younger woman feeling betrayed by her first husband, had she shown anger. She kept her feelings to herself and presented a calm exterior to the world.

Despite her husband no longer being the political leader that she had married, she was totally supportive of him. Jeremy had married the perfect woman to see him through the trouble he was facing. Rupert, their son, feels that his father would not have lasted long if his mother had not come along when she did. Marion was loyal and affectionate but also pragmatic. Unlikely to spend time dwelling on what might have been and feeling sorry for herself, life had, by now, taught her to face any future with an outward equanimity. Pauline Bessell, Peter Bessell's abandoned wife had stayed friendly with the Thorpes and stayed with them for some months in Orme Square. Writing to her husband just before he talked to the Daily Mail, she said that "Jeremy had regaled her (Pauline) with endless accounts of (Bessell's) misdeeds" and "told Marion so many different stories that even she doesn't know what to believe." If the basics of the story seem reasonably clear to us now, although Thorpe denied it all to his dying day, it was, almost forty years ago, a very confusing narrative. Marion had seen Scott in a state of hysteria and paranoia. She was far more likely to believe her smooth, articulate husband than this strange, psychologically disturbed man who was harassing him. Thorpe was extremely convincing and Marion would want to believe him and help him to cope with whatever happened in the future. She would protect this marriage vigorously.

Covert investigations continued although the Thorpes were not aware of them. Two journalists Penrose and Courtier, nicknamed Pencourt, started to investigate what Harold Wilson, who liked Jeremy despite their political differences, mistakenly believed was a South African plot to incriminate Thorpe because of his anti-apartheid stance. They did not find anything to support the South African plot but in the process of investigation found out a great deal about the Scott affair. Their findings were regularly reported in Private Eye. But elsewhere the story faded. It disappeared from the main press as other, more urgent national and interesting themes needed cover: a prolonged heatwave, the murders by the Yorkshire Ripper, IRA attacks and Queen Elizabeth II's Silver Jubilee among them. Jeremy shook off his depression and recovered his high spirits and continued his work as an MP under the new leader, David Steel. Accepted once more, he and Marion were cheered to their seats as they attended a Special Assembly of the Liberals in June. Marion offered comfort and support as did his mother Ursula. Marion, perhaps used to coping with her own mother and ex-mother-in-law, had a good relationship with this formidable woman and the two women provided a protective cushion for Jeremy against his detractors.

It is hoped that despite everything that was happening in his own life, Jeremy supported Marion when her much loved friend Benjamin Britten died. Although already very ill, in June of 1976 Britten had accepted a peerage to become Baron Britten of Aldeburgh, and it was only six months later that his heart finally failed him. It was a great sadness for Marion who had known the composer since she first arrived in London, had lived with him and his partner Pears in her teenage years, and confided in him like a brother all her adult life. The funeral was three days after his death on 7 December and he was buried in the churchyard of St Peter and St Paul at Aldeburgh. In the many photographs taken of the funeral cortege and of the churchyard by friends and the press, there is no sign of Marion or Jeremy. Despite no-one who was there being able to say for certain, it is assumed by most that she must have attended Ben's funeral. After all she was one of Britten's oldest and closest friends. It is unlikely that Jeremy was there as it was known that Britten had never liked Marion's second husband. It is most likely that she went alone and given recent publicity about Jeremy, kept a low profile.

Life settled down for some time. Marion and Jeremy established themselves for much of the time in their Devon cottage, cultivating the garden and hosting friends. Thorpe was still well-liked in the constituency and Marion too gained in popularity. Among his political work was the role of party spokesman, Chair of the UN Association and President of the Liberal Centenary Committee, set up to celebrate 100 years of the Liberal party. Typical of Jeremy, the celebration, originally intended as a fundraising exercise, ended up as a costly loss-making project. It was lavish and theatrical with a huge banquet in Birmingham, a concert by the Birmingham Symphony Orchestra and a centenary service at Westminster Abbey. Marion willingly helped as much as she could, happy with her husband's newly regained chutzpah.

But by summer 1977, the reports in Private Eye and rumours swirling around meant that Jeremy feared the story would erupt again. It did. Newton, Rinka's killer, came out of prison in October and immediately offered his story to the Evening News for £75,000 plus £25,000 extra if he was returned to prison. However, he never received such a sum as, rather naively, he also offered the paper a recording of a telephone conversation with Holmes, for just £3,000. This was enough to ignite the situation and the rest of his story and the large fee he expected were never needed. "I was hired to kill Scott," headlined the Evening News 19 October 1977. The person it was claimed had instigated the murder plan was 'a leading Liberal'. But no-one was in any doubt who this person was. The article also revealed that DCS Michael Challes of Avon and Somerset Police had been asked to undertake an investigation into the alleged plot.

Marion and Jeremy returned to London from Devon to face the coming furore of speculation. Jeremy looked grim but calm as they arrived at Orme Square but Marion was able to keep him calm and focussed with her strong, supportive manner.

The Liberal party were appalled, Bessell once again was in his element and gave even more interviews to the press. After two weeks of more revelations, Jeremy called a Press conference. Hordes of journalists converged on the venue, the former Scotland Yard building which had become an annexe of the House of Commons. They then learned the venue had been changed to the Gladstone Library of the national Liberal Club. Facing the eighty-two journalists (and the two Pencourt journalists who had climbed in through the rafters) were Jeremy, Marion, John Montgomerie (the partner of Thorpe's lawyer Lord Goodman) and Clement Freud. A long rebuttal statement by Thorpe ended with a plea for the press to relieve the intolerable strain on 'my wife, my family and me' and a statement that he had no intention of resigning and had not received a single request to do so from his constituency association. He sat down, putting his arm round Marion.

Then there were questions. A BBC reporter Keith Graves asked, "the whole of this hinges on your private life. It is necessary to ask if you have ever had a homosexual relationship?" Marion stood up and angrily shouted, "Go on, stand up." "Stand up and say that again." Graves did, and calmly repeated the question "Would you comment on rumours that you have had a homosexual relationship". Before Thorpe could answer or Marion could remonstrate again, Montgomerie interjected to say that he could not allow his client to answer the question. In the hubbub following with everyone shouting, Jeremy and Marion left by a back staircase.

I find it strange that Marion asked the question in the press conference, or that she ever believed that her husband had not had homosexual relationships. There was ample evidence that she could not possibly have failed to read or hear. It is much more believable that she knew, quite rightly, that Jeremy loved her and that she hoped that his relationships with men were in the past. Jeremy's homosexuality was not on trial, it had been fully legal for over ten years by this time. Fellow politicians with a similar past had either 'come out' or it did not matter anymore. An accusation of conspiracy to murder was a different thing. Marion fully accepted her husband's assurance that he was not involved in any plot to silence Scott, and particularly she could not believe that he was the sort of man to condone murder, an opinion shared by those family and friends who knew him well. Perhaps the outburst was her attempt to protect her husband. But calling the press conference had been a mistake. It led to even more speculation and renewed press interest.

Marion had to cope with Thorpe's changing moods. At times, reported his colleagues, he seemed half-crazed with despair, but carried out his normal duties with calm aplomb. He was drinking heavily. In May 1978, although the Challes report was some months off, Lord Goodman learned through the legal grapevine that Jeremy was going to be charged. He arranged that Sir David Napley, a brilliant defence solicitor, would represent his friend. After interviewing all those involved, Challes delivered his report to the Director of Public Prosecutions, Sam Silkin. At the end of July on the advice of the DPP, Silkin decided that the prosecution would go ahead. And on August 8, four men, Jeremy Thorpe, David Holmes, John Le Mesurier and George Deakin presented themselves at different times at Minehead police station where they were charged with conspiring to murder Norman Scott. Additionally, Thorpe was charged with having incited Holmes to murder Scott in 1969. That afternoon they were bailed to appear in the magistrates' court on 12 September 1978 for the committal trial. This would decide whether the case was one which would proceed to the Crown Court.

The uncertainty of whether there would be a committal had gone and somehow Jeremy seemed relieved. As before he drank a lot but friends reported he seemed jaunty and when with them he discussed the preparation for his coming appearance with some enthusiasm. Although he had agreed with David Steel that he would resign if charged, he decided not to, as this might be seen a sign of guilt. He was staunchly supported, at least in public, by local Liberals and announced his intention to stand at the autumn election on 5 October. Jim Callaghan, the then Labour Prime Minister decided not to call an autumn election after all, which was seen as a disappointment for the Liberals. They knew that now they would have to fight the next election in the aftermath of the trial. Typical of Jeremy, and no doubt agreed with Marion, he made a theatrical appearance at the Liberal assembly on the 14 September to a mixed reception of applause and silence.

It had been a stressful summer for them both. Marion, as ever a keen traveller, took Jeremy off for a three-week holiday in Morocco, much needed by both, before they returned to plan his defence. Napley had retained the QC George Carman, to represent Jeremy. The barrister was part of the Northern Circuit and based in Manchester, and not well-known in London, nevertheless Napley felt that Carman's skill in cross-examining and his persuasiveness would suit the case. Carman, was delighted to have been briefed for 'the case of the century'. Committal proceedings began at Minehead 20 November 1978 and lasted for three weeks. Reporters descended on the small town in droves. Napley and his wife moved in with Marion and Jeremy at Cobbaton. The cottage was constantly besieged by the press and entrances to the property were blocked, Marion was very angry with the press intrusion but had to bear it. Her husband was news. Always generous with her time and hospitality, she managed the house full of lawyers and advisers with her usual aplomb. Sadly, Marion was far too involved in the committal proceedings to attend the unveiling of the memorial stone to Benjamin Britten in the north choir (Musicians) of Westminster Abbey on 21 November. She would surely have enjoyed the occasion as Britten's old friend, composer Sir Lennox Berkeley, unveiled it during a concert of Britten's music.

But Marion had much more pressing things on her mind. On Monday morning 20 November the proceedings began. To the surprise of all Jeremy's supporters, Deakin's solicitor asked for reporting restrictions to be removed. The law at the time allowed any of the accused unilaterally to lift any previous ban. Against Thorpe's wishes, the case would now be splashed across the press in lurid headlines. Marion gasped, visibly shocked. Her husband showed no emotion as he sat alone at the front of the court as far as possible from his co-defendants, "looking for all the world as if he was listening to a debate in the house of commons." The whole story was laid bare to the magistrates in all its lurid detail. Many of his erstwhile friends and supporters now felt that they had not been told the truth or at best that Jeremy had not confided in them. Marion and Jeremy's mother Ursula, both dressed smartly, sat every day in the front row of the public gallery, firmly determined to show support. However, even they had only previously heard Jeremy's side of the story and read the limited press reports. They too now had far more information about his intimate relationships. Despite any preparation for the revelations, they must have been a shock to both women. A news report filmed on the 24 November shows Jeremy and Marion leaving the court in their white Rover car, some supporters reaching in to shake hands, and then the couple walking along the sea front at Minehead, talking to a reporter. When arriving or leaving court, aware of being photographed, Marion smiles, although the smile seems fixed. As they walk Marion has her arm linked into Jeremy's and looks on, again smiling, as her husband answers questions. She says nothing. The reporter comments on how much strain Jeremy must be experiencing and asks what the couple will be doing for the weekend. Despite answers to the reporter being affable and calm - Jeremy says he is going to see if any constituents need help, go to church and walk in the fresh air - he also explains about the strain on his family of relentless press attention. If it is like the last weekend he says, when the press surrounded the church and staked out the cottage, he and Marion would have to stay in the garden.

From the confusion of evidence and information they had heard, they were confident that the case, at least against Jeremy, would be thrown out. Others were less surprised after everything that had been alleged at the committal. On the 13 December 1978, the Minehead magistrates decided that there was a prima facie case against all the defendants and committed them for trial. Marion put a hand to her mouth, stifling her shock. Jeremy blinked rapidly and moved his jaw slowly from side to side.

Marion now had more knowledge of her husband and his past than she could possibly have wanted. Most wives would be forgiven, even praised, for heading straight to the divorce courts. But Marion was not like most wives. Some people, faced with extreme adversity, develop a strength of character that sustains them and Marion was such a person. She had coped with adversity before. She decided where her loyalties lay and never wavered from her support for Thorpe and her belief in his innocence, at least of any criminal act. The Thorpes were appalled at the verdict. Jeremy continued to drink heavily and occasionally he exhibited slurred speech and an unsteady gait when he had not been drinking. These were possibly the early symptoms of a later diagnosed Parkinson's disease, brought on by the stress of his situation.[91]

Although both his solicitor Napley and his QC Carman gave their professional services for relatively little, knowing that this case, win or lose, would give them maximum publicity, other costs would be enormous. There were still supporters who believed in him. Lord Lloyd of Kilgerran, a rich patent lawyer who had paid the expenses of Jeremy's private office when he was leader, set up a Jeremy Thorpe Defence Fund. His mother Ursula sold the upper floor of her house to its sitting tenants to raise money and Marion sold some of the things she had received as part of her divorce settlement to contribute to the fund.

That winter of 1978-79 was hard in Britain, a 'winter of discontent'. The period from November to February was characterised by widespread pay strikes by both public and private sector trade unions. It was exacerbated by the coldest winter weather in sixteen years and the public in some areas suffered great inconvenience with rubbish piling up on streets, hospital entrances blockaded and bodies remaining unburied. The Labour Prime minister James Callaghan refused to acknowledge the severity of the situation, leading to the Sun headline 'Crisis? What Crisis?' Margaret Thatcher, the leader of the Conservatives spoke of the severity of the situation in a party-political broadcast in the same week.

Despite the strain of the impending trial, Thorpe continued to carry out his parliamentary duties. He was one of the Liberals who spoke at a meeting and voted with colleagues to side with the Conservatives to bring down the Labour government. On 28 March a vote of no confidence in the Callaghan government was won by one vote, 311 to 310. Supposedly, Mrs Thatcher led a conga of her supporters through the corridors of the Commons to celebrate. A general election was called for May. Unfortunately, the election was set for the fourth day of Thorpe's trial, 3 May, and against his agent's advice he accepted the invitation of the North Devon Liberals to stand, once again, as their candidate. Because of the impending election he managed to get the date of the trial postponed until later in May. All through April Marion and Ursula campaigned heroically for Jeremy in his Devon constituency but although many of his local supporters seemed loyal, the Party in Westminster distanced itself from him. He tried hard and made some good speeches but his jovial manner had gone and he seemed strained. He confessed to Marion and close friends that he did not expect to win. His campaign was not helped by Auberon Waugh who, for many years was a thorn in his side writing for Private Eye. Waugh decided to stand as the 'dog lovers' candidate. Waugh's pre-election address in the Spectator included "Rinka is not forgotten. Rinka lives. Woof, woof." Eventually a claim by Thorpe's lawyers for an injunction was granted by the Court of Appeal and the address was removed. But the damage had been done and Waugh remained a candidate.

In the General Election of 1979, Thorpe lost his parliamentary seat, a seat he had held for twenty years, to the Conservatives by 8,473 votes. Auberon Waugh polled 79. Although there was a large swing to the Conservatives everywhere, the Liberals did much worse in the West

Country than the rest of England, neighbouring Liberal MPs also losing their seats. This was blamed on Jeremy, and was known as the Thorpe Effect. Jeremy appeared stunned at losing even although for most people the result was inevitable. He and Marion invited the press who had been a fixture outside throughout the committal trial, into the house on the morning after his defeat. He sipped whisky and Marion sat by his side smoking and showing little emotion. He referred to his loss as shattering and defended his record in supporting his constituency. He appealed to Marion to confirm this. He seemed genuinely shocked that he had not been understood. He was no longer The King of Devon.

On Tuesday 8 May 1979, Marion's husband, an ex-MP, a man no longer with a role in politics, took his place in the huge glass-walled dock of the Old Bailey.

FIFTEEN

The Trial

The great success of the Conservatives at the election had issued in a new era. Margaret Thatcher, the 'Iron Lady' was in power. It was the beginning of a period of tough conservatism that increased privatisation and reduced the power and influence of the trade unions. The Liberals had been pushed to the margins of political life, no longer newsworthy. Except, that is, for one Liberal who was at the centre of the news for six weeks, Marion's husband, Jeremy Thorpe. Just five days after the general election, the four alleged conspirators appeared in Court No. 1 at the Old Bailey and the trial for conspiracy to murder Norman Scott began.

Marion was now needed as never before to keep her husband calm and positive. It must have been a shock for her. The man she had married, the politician that many thought would eventually be part of a government, was now a potential criminal. Much of his past had been laid bare and he was facing what could be a long prison sentence if found guilty. But Marion never considered her husband guilty of being involved in planning a murder. Perhaps she accepted that he had had homosexual relationships; it would be difficult not to as there was so much evidence. She may have accepted some of Scott's story too, at least the story of a close friendship. But conspiracy to murder? No!

She was fiercely loyal to her husband. She had fought for her first marriage until she could not resist divorce, and she would fight to maintain her new one. On day one of the trial Jeremy strode into court accompanied by Marion and his uncle, Air Marshall Peter Norton-Griffiths, a distinguished ex-military officer and barrister. Marion and Jeremy's mother Ursula decided to present a united front. Marion could be as formidable as her mother-in law. A photograph of the couple arriving at court later in the trial shows a rather depressed looking Thorpe preceded by the imposing, well-groomed figure of Marion striding purposefully ahead, rather like Mrs Thatcher, handbag at the ready. Together the two women attended each day of the trial, dressed 'as if for a day at the races' and sat in the front row of the public seats. Marion seemed to listen intently to the evidence and to enjoy the proceedings. According to Bessell who was to be a witness, Jeremy looked terrible. "Now, deathly pale, huddled in a dark overcoat, he was half-slumped on the upright wooden chair in that vast edifice; a defeated man staring into space."[92] On the other hand, Bessel noticed how good Marion looked. She was "no longer the overweight housewife with a garish artificial white streak in her black hair, she was slimmer, surprisingly relaxed and far more attractive."[93]

The judge, Sir Joseph Cantley was sixty-eight and was regarded as competent and conventional. He was known for making witty or sarcastic remarks and for being something of a snob. He was very aware he was trying a national figure with a distinguished record. Impatient with the 'lesser mortals' among the crown witnesses, Bessell, Scott and Newton, his behaviour at the trial gave rise to a view that he was biased in favour of the defence. This view was to become more prevalent as the case progressed.

The outline of the case followed a similar path as the Committal. There was nothing much new. However, when the prosecution case began, it was a different story. The witnesses were relentlessly interrogated by Carman, using all his skill to get the witnesses to say what he wanted them to say. The three main witnesses were worn down by questions. Bessell, after three days agreed that he was a habitual liar but collected himself at the end of the interrogation to assert "If I were no longer capable of being believed, I would not be here at the Old Bailey, I would be at Oceanside, California." Scott was rattled by the inference that he had been the predator. Newton, although cocky and not at all cowed by questions, found that his insistence that he had been hired to kill and not just to frighten Scott was contradicted by others. He was also forced to admit that he had told a pack of lies at his own trial and that he was 'out to milk the case' for all it was worth. The Judge, who saw himself as a 'wag' ridiculed some of the witnesses if they faltered or seemed to be finding it difficult to cope with the questioning. The witnesses tended to contradict each other.

The prosecuting Counsel Peter Taylor was sympathetic to Jeremy even though it was his job to prosecute. He made an agreement with Carman not to expose the details of

Thorpe's sex life, and not to call on witnesses who claimed to have had affairs with him, but only if Jeremy admitted to having had 'homosexual tendencies' at one point in his life. This admittance was slipped in, and its innocuous nature certainly avoided what would have been sensational headlines.

The defence case opened on June 9 – and ended there. Carman rose to say he would not call any evidence on behalf of Holmes, Le Mesurier or Thorpe. None of these three defendants would be called. Jeremy would have gone into the witness box but it had been decided that he would not help his case if he rose to the occasion as he usually did and came over as over-confident and theatrical. Only Deakin was called who always insisted that he had been asked by Holmes and Mesurier to find someone to frighten Scott and not to kill him. The evidence seemed contradictory.

The final address to the jury by each representative of the four accused men summarised the defence. The QCs sought to draw attention to their client's good character where possible or to their lack of intelligence to be involved in such a complex plot. Carman, in defending Jeremy appealed for their pity for a man who had gone through so much. He mentioned the death of Caroline, Thorpe's first wife, and referred admiringly to Marion, "whose constant presence in this court speaks eloquently for itself."

On 18 June, Judge Cantley began his summing up. It has been suggested that the judge was extremely biased in favour of the defence and particularly Jeremy. He criticised Bessell as a humbug because he was a lay preacher at the same time as being sexually promiscuous, he called Scott a "hysterical, warped personality, accomplished sponger and very skilful at exploiting sympathy." To add to this he concluded, "He is a crook… he is a fraud. He is a sponger. He is a whiner. He is a parasite. But of course, he could still be telling the truth". Newton was dismissed as a 'chump' for bungling the plot and Deakin and Mesurier were briefly dealt with by arguing that there were contradictions in evidence relating to them.

The Jury retired for two full days. Jeremy could not go home with Marion. As their bail was withdrawn when the jury retired, the four men, were taken to Brixton Jail. The first night, Jeremy complained of a stomach upset and spent the night in the prison hospital. Auberon Waugh, following the trial closely for Private Eye could not resist a dig at Thorpe.

"Thursday. (21 May) The jury is still out. Thorpe apparently spent the night in hospital in Brixton prison with a stomach upset. Just occasionally, I have suffered from an upset stomach and it can be quite disagreeable, although it has never occurred to me to go to hospital for it.

The other three defendants, being of a lower class, spent the night locked in a single cell. Although not by nature a left-winger, I feel something in this case stirs the latent Robespierre in me."

The following day they waited for the verdict and, relieved that things were about to come to an end and after the judge's summing up they were fairly hopeful that they would win, they joked and played cards together. After another day of the jury's deliberations, (it was revealed later that this day was spent persuading the twelfth juror to agree to acquit all four of the accused), the men spent one more night in Brixton, sharing a cell.

The jurors, as they afterwards admitted, were deeply impressed by the argument that witnesses had been paid to ensure a conviction. And one of them had decided for 'not guilty' because he was touched by the constancy of Marion Thorpe.[94]

At half-past two on Friday 22 June 1979 the jury announced a 'not guilty' verdict for all the accused. Jeremy beamed, tossed the red cushions he had been using over the dock, leaned over and kissed Marion.

"Darling, we won."

FIVE

SIXTEEN

Wilderness

Jeremy was delighted with the verdict and flung his arms in the air in victory. He came out of court alongside Marion and reiterated his innocence to the waiting press. He thanked his wife and his family for their support. Back at Orme Square the couple opened the champagne and Jeremy appeared on the balcony with a beaming Marion, his mother and Rupert. Very like Royalty they acknowledged the crowd and posed for photographs. What the ordinary public, passing by on Bayswater Road must have made of what looked like unknown royals waving at them from a balcony, is anyone's guess. But Jeremy and Marion were on a high. They held a victory party for his lawyers and their family and friends inside the house. The couple were delighted that it was all over.

But it was not.

Throughout the trial and for some time afterwards, the Press hounded Marion and Jeremy. Friends such as Iona and Robin Salinger were followed and asked for comment, which they refused. Journalists and photographers camped outside Orme Square when the couple were in residence, blocking the entrance and forcing the family to resort to subterfuge to escape from the house through a back entrance. One day, James and Jeremy, two of Marion's teenage sons, then long-haired and clean-shaven, dressed as women and went out to divert the crowd. The reporters ogled and touched them, an experience James said made them realise what women had to put up with. Reporters followed the couple to Devon too, attempting to block the two entrances, uphill and downhill to their cottage. Marion had experienced two sides of Press intrusion; the somewhat sycophantic coverage of her life when she was a young woman, and now the disagreeable type. She hated it.

Still high after the verdict, and no doubt very relieved with the result, the couple went to stay at Cobbaton for the weekend. There they received congratulations from the local Liberal party who wanted to nominate him again as their parliamentary candidate. The local constituency Liberals threw a coffee evening for 200 people. One local vicar, the Rev John Hornby, a colourful character and a strong supporter of Jeremy decided to hold a service of thanksgiving for the acquittal. The vicar was sure that so many well-wishers would want to come to his old church at Bratton Fleming, that he arranged for the service to be relayed to the expected overflow congregation in the village hall. Jeremy was enthusiastic. Others were not. To bring God into the decision to acquit Jeremy was too uncomfortable a link for most people, and apart from Marion, Jeremy and Rupert in the front pew and a few curious local people, the small congregation at the service consisted mainly of journalists, about eighty of them. The village hall stood empty. Undeterred, the vicar continued with his unctuous praise. He attributed the Thorpe's endurance of their ordeal to divine intervention. "In the long dark days of Minehead and the Old Bailey, God granted Marion and Jeremy that fantastic resilience which has aroused the resilience of the whole world!... Thanks be to God, for with God nothing is impossible."[95] This was too much for the Archdeacon of Barnstaple, Ronald Herniman. He called it unfitting, unseemly and unsavoury. Like many others, he had found the trial result unsatisfactory. "There is a great deal of unhappiness about the result at the Old Bailey. As far as most people are concerned, the trial ended with a big question mark over the case."[96]

Although the Devon Liberals appeared to support him, his Parliamentary colleagues were lukewarm. A statement by David Steel as leader and on behalf of the Liberal party welcomed the verdict as a great relief and expressed his hope that Thorpe would eventually find avenues where his talents could be used. It was clear that such avenues for these talents would not be opened up by the Liberals. The Party did not want him back. According to her friend Iona Salinger, Marion felt that the Liberal Party let her husband down and she was angry at how he was treated by it in the ensuing years.

However, she was regarded as having behaved impeccably during the trial. Like the vicar of Bratton Fleming, John Hornby, and QC Carman, all of whom had applauded her support for her husband, there were many others too that admired Marion's resilience. She was coping with a situation she could never have expected when she married Thorpe. She firmly believed in the verdict given by the jury. Jeremy was innocent as far as she was concerned, whatever she felt about the evidence against the other three accused men.

But to the wider world, the evidence produced had discredited Thorpe. By many he was considered lucky to have 'got off.' There was both serious and amused reaction to the way that the judge had summed up the case. In late June, only a week after the end of the trial, one of a series of shows, The Secret Policeman's Ball, was held at her Majesty's Theatre in aid of Amnesty. The show must have been seen as treason by Jeremy who had been a founder of the charity, many years before. Peter Cook, the comedian and satirist, delivered a nine-minute parody of Judge Cantley's summing-up of the Thorpe trial. *Entirely a Matter for You*, still available on Youtube. Even today, it is a devastating and wickedly funny sketch, and, according to those who attended the trial, not too far from reality. It is obvious from the delight of the large audience that night, mostly young people, that the idea that there had been a travesty of justice had become part of the nation's view of the proceedings. The well-reported judge's summing up, whilst it might have influenced the jury in a way favourable to Jeremy at the time, was seen as indicative of a snobbish bias in favour of a member of the upper classes. This judge's opinion did Jeremy no favours after the trial; it raised the strong suspicion that there could have been a wrong decision by the jury. Private Eye had a field day at the expense of the couple. The front page of the magazine, the 'Grand Acquittal Souvenir' on 6 July shows them waving to the crowd, Marion clutching her long gloves and beaming, Jeremy lifting his hat in the air triumphantly. But the speech balloon superimposed on the photo of Jeremy are "Buggers can't be losers", and the balloon over Marion reads, "You lucky sod".

Despite Jeremy's initial euphoria and his hope that he might be able to resume his political career, his close friends Clement Freud and Lord Avebury, both who had remained loyal, persuaded him that any attempt for a political comeback would be unsuccessful, at least for the near future. Opinions on his downfall and of his character by other politicians of the time, still varied. Barbara Castle, the Labour MP commented that he had been brought down by inadequacies of his personality. Cyril Smith, a fellow Liberal MP said he "had paid one hell of a price."

He certainly had in his political life.

The couple had to endure the steady flow of books and articles about Jeremy and the trial, including the reminiscences of Peter Bessell and of David Holmes. He was encouraged not to sue David Holmes by political adviser Lord Goodman. But the failure to bring a libel action against Holmes was held against him by both members of his party and the public, and once again led to doubts about whether the result of the trial had been correct.

He still felt that Devon was his political base. Jeremy kept his house at Cobbaton and he and Marion spent more time there and continued to support the local Liberals in his old Devon constituency. However, there was a sense that even the old timers thought of him as a figure from the past. A collection to reward him for his twenty years of service as an MP resulted in only £1000. Marion and he spent it on an ornamental bridge across their duckpond at the cottage.

Cobbaton was a refuge in the months after the trial, but six months later Jeremy emerged to face what seemed a hostile world. Marion, Jeremy and Rupert attended a fundraising concert for the United Nations Human Rights Day and the International Year of the Child. Journalists who attended the event at the parish church of Buckingham Palace in Belgravia wrote derogatory comments about Jeremy. One, writing in the Evening Standard 11 December commented, "Thorpe's spirit, once his personal trademark, seemed to flicker to life only infrequently and his bitterness appeared to weigh like a coat of lead.... His features were immobile, his eyes wide open and blinking like two round marbles set in plasticine." Jeremy was certainly bitter about how he had been treated, especially by the press. But his set features which only occasionally changed expression, were not only due to his discontent but also to the beginning of the illness, yet undisclosed to the public, which would devastate his future life.

As though a trial for conspiracy to murder and political annihilation was not enough for one year, it was in 1979 that Jeremy was diagnosed with Parkinson's disease. The stress of exposure by Scott that he had suffered for so many years had most likely triggered the symptoms of the disease. The occasional fixed expression on his face during the trial had not been the result of drinking heavily or depression as many had thought, but early, typical symptoms of Parkinson's. He first noticed that doing up his shirt buttons was difficult and that it brought on a feeling of nausea. Marion and he had to cope with the knowledge of his diagnosis for some years until the symptoms became more obvious and his illness was made public. It must have been a very difficult thing for the fit, dapper Jeremy to accept. He was beginning to shake, his impaired balance resulted in falls which sometimes required hospitalisation, his handwriting deteriorated and his much-admired speaking voice began to fail. However, his intellect remained unimpaired and from this time until he died, he was as active as ever mentally. Despite people thinking that due to his increasingly immobility of feature and unblinking eyes he had sunk into a depression and become inactive, he was keen to seek a new career. He and Marion agreed that to publicise his condition could detract from his chances of such a career and it was only in the mid 1980s that it became public knowledge.

Hopes that Marion and Jeremy had for his return to political life were soon dashed. Jack Hayward had been considerably shaken by the allegation in the trial that unbeknown to him, his contributions to the Liberal cause might have been used to pay a would-be murderer. Now he demanded that the Liberal Party investigate the matter. Eventually Hayward agreed to let the matter drop if Thorpe repaid the money. But the Liberals were rattled, some wanting Jeremy expelled from the party and some even suggesting he be prosecuted for being unable to account for the money. It was not the accusations of homosexuality or his possible complicity in a murder plan that had most upset his erstwhile political allies, it was Thorpe's seemingly cavalier attitude to other people's money. The suggestion of prosecution was rejected by David Steele, the Leader of the Party, but there was now no chance that Thorpe could resume any sort of political career. He was yesterday's man to them.

Obtaining work proved extremely difficult. Few employers wanted to take on such a so recently notorious figure. He thought first of television where he had sparkled in the 1950s and 60s but despite some auditions, his applications came to nothing. His charisma was no longer evident; because of his developing illness he appeared wooden. He had a good knowledge of Central Africa so thought of trying to play a role in the transition of Rhodesia to Zimbabwe. Again, this failed, as the British Governor. Lord Soames did not want to be associated with him and Jeremy had been on the side of Mugabe's rivals in the past. Then in 1982 what might have seemed an ideal post became available, that of Director of the British wing of Amnesty International. Jeremy had been one of Amnesty's founders in 1961and had a solid record of supporting human rights. However, his notoriety, his questionable financial dealings and his lack of administrative experience brought an avalanche of opposition. He ended it by withdrawing his application. This was a great disappointment to Marion who had thought the post ideal for her husband's skills and interests. To her, this was yet another example of a lack of loyalty; a quality which she valued highly.

Only just into his fifties, Jeremy Thorpe was at a loss as to where his future career lay.

Marion, only a few years older than her husband, must also have reflected on her situation as the new decade began. Once again, her life had taken a new direction. She had changed her country and nationality as a young girl, she had given up a musical career, she had gone from being a countess with a country estate to a single mother in London. She had been the wife of a successful politician, a politician who had expected an increasingly high profile and possibly a place in government. She had lost her close friend and confidante Benjamin Britten. But all that was past. But now?

The couple was no longer part of the political life of the country. Although Jeremy had been acquitted of any wrongdoing that is not how the general public saw it. For a short time, Marion had to bear the ridicule, negative publicity and intrusion into her family life. But Marion was still Marion. At core she was a wife, a mother, a musician, a musicologist. She could cope. Unlike her husband she had many calls on her time. Despite her concern for her husband, for his health and his spirits, she had plenty of other things to do. Marion's three older sons were now making their own ways in life. Whatever their private opinions they had accepted their mother's choice of new husband and supported the couple when needed. Although Orme Square was still their London base, one by one they moved out into their own homes. But Rupert, Jeremy's son and the stepson Marion had mothered since 1973, was still only nine or ten when press interest was at its height around the time of the trial. Marion and Jeremy needed to protect him. Rupert remembers being photographed on the way to school, which he found quite exciting. This may possibly have led to an interest much later, in press photography as a career. But his parents wanted to keep him away from such publicity at such a young age so he was taken out of his school in London and tutored down in Devon by local teachers. His parents were successful in maintaining as much normality as possible for him, and it was not until many years later that he understood what had gone on during his childhood. At the time there was no discussion with him about what was happening. It was not the sort of family who sat down together to discuss its plans. At about the age of ten, he was sent to a crammer in the Cotswolds, again to protect him from what was going on in London but also probably to prepare him for the common entrance exam the following year. Although the boarding school was in a lovely part of the country, the school was a disaster for Rupert. He hated it. It was, he says, full of 'thick rich kids' and he was a rarity there in not having a title. Lessons were every day except Sunday afternoon and the boys were hit with a bat if they did anything out of line. He was relieved therefore when after a year, Jeremy and Marion decided to transfer him to Frensham Heights School near Farnham in Surrey. It was an inspired choice. The headmaster dispensed with the need for an entrance exam pass. The school emphasised then, and still does, a caring community, the curriculum being delivered flexibly to suit the child. The school focussed on the needs of each individual child rather than on strict guidelines and Rupert loved it. It was co-ed and even though a boarding school it was homely. He did not always want to go home to London at weekends, preferring to spend time in the schools well-equipped dark room on his photography, which he soon decided would be his future career. He became a very successful photographer living and working in the USA. After his schooldays, when he was working at early jobs in London, he lived again at Orme Square.

The house was, for him, amazing. It might have been the perfect house for his father when an aspiring politician, but it was also a wonderful place for a teenager. He remembers hosting crazy parties there when his parents were away in Devon; moving all the furniture and carpets and having smoke machines, loud music and DJs. In his twenties, early in the 1990s he moved out of the big house into his own London flat.

Over the years the Orme Square house became less smart but always welcoming. Marion was not house proud, the house was for living in and entertaining others, not for show. Although there was money available to maintain it "Marion never spent a dime on the house," said Rupert. Not quite true, he corrected himself. She would have things done on the cheap and then need to have them redone, costing more. She would not put the heating on until mid-December, maybe from the memory of growing up in wartime conditions. Whilst always smart when she needed to be on show, she bought clothes locally, sometimes at Whiteleys, the department store round the corner in Queensway and her summer clothes often came from Aldeburgh.

Rupert loved Orme Square and was happy too in his father's cottage at Cobbaton. Whilst at Frensham Heights he returned to Devon for most of his holidays and was equally at home there. Marion and Jeremy too spent more of their time at the cottage where the family and close friends were welcomed. By the early 1980s, Marion had eight or nine small grandchildren and the number was growing. Sophie, her eldest grandchild, the daughter of her son James, was a regular visitor to the cottage and she was close to Rupert; and still is. They are only a few years apart in age. They grew up together. Sophie remembers that after her parents parted when she was eight, she spent time staying with both James, her father, and Frederica her mother. As her parents travelled a lot, her father a musician and her mother a stage designer, Marion's homes became a base for Sophie. Although her grandmother could seem cold to people who did not know her, this was a protective front. Marion was a warm and affectionate woman says Sophie. She loved games and to play with the children. Sophie remembers her grandmother singing over and over to her to lull her to sleep. Jeremy became a much-loved grandpa, with a fund of stories. Marion always had music in the house, and taught Sophie, who enjoyed classical music, to play the piano.

Easters were often spent at the cottage in Devon and some Christmases were spent there. There were big family gatherings at Curlews, Marion's house just north of Aldeburgh. It too was a much-used meeting place for all the family. It is surprising to Sophie looking back that so many people could be accommodated in both houses. Ben Britten and Peter Pears were close by in Aldeburgh, and James and his family lived for a time at Church Farm in nearby Sotherton. Marion's other sons and their families came often. Curlews was sold some time in the 1980s when Marion and Jeremy no longer needed it. But they kept their links with Aldeburgh and the area for the rest of their lives.

Marion and Jeremy were still members of the community in the village of Chittlehampton. Although perhaps not quite as visible there socially as previously. Marion occasionally went to church at St. James's in Swimbridge with Jeremy and Rupert. The vicar at that time, Nigel Jackson-Stevens remembers that driving round the narrow country lanes and coping with oncoming traffic proved difficult for Marion. He remembered having to step in to reverse her open-topped car in the lanes around Cobbaton. "Reversing wasn't her forte!" he laughed.

SEVENTEEN

Reconnecting

Marion was very hospitable, as was her husband. Many friends came to stay at Orme Square Almost everyone in the family seems to have spent time living at the cottage or in the flat there at some time in their lives. Jeremy's devoted secretary Judy Young, who remained with him until he died, lived in the basement flat. Marion opened her house to any friends and family who needed accommodation in London. When James's first marriage ended in 1985, he lived with Marion and Jeremy for a time; a stay which was extended later when he remarried. Jeremy's young cousin Christina Morgan came to stay for a year while she studied at a London art college in 1980. Christina stayed close to Jeremy and Marion and when Christina and her two sisters married in a triple wedding in Normandy, the trip to France was just one of the Thorpe's trips abroad. In the early 1980s, the couple travelled extensively both for holidays and in connection with Jeremy's projects. Jeremy did not need to bring in an income thanks to the financial backing of an elderly bachelor admirer based in Luxembourg but he kept busy. He remained Chair of the United Nations Association, supported various charities and got involved in (mostly eccentric and unsuccessful) business projects. He and Marion were now firmly a devoted married couple. There were no more rumours about his homosexuality and she no longer, if she ever did, wondered about how he spent his time when away from her. As his illness developed, they spent most of their time together and he relied on Marion increasingly as his unobtrusive carer. The couple could often be seen at recitals at Wigmore Hall, "Jeremy a gaunt skeletal figure debilitated by Parkinson's, and Marion focused on his needs."[97]

Music still had a key part in Marion's life. She continued her links with Suffolk and particularly Aldeburgh and the Aldeburgh Festival, held each June, was a 'must attend' for her and as many family members who could go for many years. Although her long and very close friendship with Benjamin Britten had ended with his death in 1976, her relationship with Ben's partner, Peter Pears, was equally enduring, and remained until he died ten years later. Marion kept in touch with him as a friend. Postcards from holidays, a key feature of communication with Ben and Peter in the past, continued. In summer 1977, Marion sent a postcard of Sicily to Peter, "Thinking of you". In the same month Peter, now holidaying alone just a few months after the death of Ben, wrote to Marion. He was "visiting gently my old acquaintances in Tuscany." Visits to Aldeburgh and Snape Maltings concert hall continued to be part of her life and she enjoyed meeting old friends, especially musicians such as Murray Perahia and Mstislav and Galina

Rostropovich, there. Jeremy often accompanied her until his attendance became impossible due to his illness. One such concert, arranged to celebrate Peter Pears's seventieth birthday, featured Perahia and Rostropovich (Slava) on the programme. During the course of the evening, Perahia appeared on stage to announce that Rostropovich apologised for not being able to fly from America to perform, due to other commitments, but that he had sent his most promising pupil to play on his behalf. "The most drab-looking woman in a faded green dress, straw hat and never-to-be forgotten plastic shoes appeared on the stage. She sat down to polite applause and after what seemed like an eternity, took off her hat, started to unbutton her dress and lo, underneath, dressed in a dinner jacket, was Rostropovich!"[98] Marion, knowing Slava's mischievous sense of humour, would probably have been in on the joke.

Marion became chair of the Britten Pears Foundation and also a trustee of the Britten-Pears School for Advanced Musical Studies, set up in 1977 just after Britten died. The school offered a programme of training for young musicians and singers, a cause Marion always supported. She and her fellow trustees had to treat Pears with care if they wanted to make any changes; Peter considered the school to be his and Britten's baby. He could get angry and tearful if he thought his teaching and judgement had been called into question. Marion's tact and her closeness to him helped to smooth some difficult situations. In 1985, just a year before the singer died, Pears celebrated his seventy-fifth birthday. Marion edited a Festschrift, a tribute to Pears, published by Faber Music Limited in association with the

Britten Estate. It was kept a secret until a beautifully bound copy was presented to Peter on his birthday.

Her own personal contribution is well written and with humour. She thanked him for the pleasure he had given her in his repertoire: Schubert, Schumann, Mozart, Bach, Handel, Purcell, Mahler and folk songs, and added that she found it difficult to appreciate them sung by others. Later in the tribute she thanked him too for pieces special to her; for *Dalla sua pace* (alas never on the stage), *Nacht und Traume,* for Flute and Grimes, for the Evangelist – and then adds a light note. "Oh dear, one should never start naming names, although I don't think you would ever react like the famous violinist, who, when praised for his playing of a particular movement of a work, retorted: 'And what was wrong with the rest of it?'

To finish, she remembered her the years she spent living with Peter and with Ben and especially, "The privilege of having shared with you and Ben the excitement of planning and achieving so many great musical events is something very precious."

After Pears died, Marion remained involved with Aldeburgh and the Red House. However, now she was married to Jeremy, her relationships with others who were involved with the future of the Red House were not always easy. Jeremy tended to ruffle feathers. "I think the problem with Jeremy was that he always wanted to dominate conversations (when he was still up to it) but never seemed to take anything seriously, said one. He was very demanding of Marion, and the more he deteriorated the more he asked of her - but she never complained or commented on his behaviour." It must have been very difficult for a man like Jeremy, who had once been a persuasive and eloquent speaker to no longer to be regarded as important as a leader and decision maker. Marion had been used to staying at the Red House for many years as in a friend's home, and she and Jeremy, and other trustees and their families continued to use it when they were in Suffolk. At Marion's instigation, to modernise the accommodation, the big bedroom at the front of the house, where she and Jeremy stayed, was changed to accommodate a bathroom. The kitchen was changed into a dining room with the former pantry becoming the new kitchen. Unfortunately, the considerations of the house's future as a museum, as an accurate picture of the house in Britten's time, were not considered fully at the time. Many of the changes have now been reversed to restore authenticity. By the turn of the century, other trustees were keen that the modernised house be used to accommodate musicians, writers, painters and administrators over the festival period. Marion and Jeremy's use of it had to be limited. The couple no longer had Curlews as an alternative. Marion accepted these changes with relatively good grace, but Jeremy was very annoyed at being 'banished'.

Although 1985 was a good year with the Peter Pears celebrations, festivals and trips abroad, it was also the year when Jeremy's illness could no longer be hidden. He and Marion announced it to the outside world. Jeremy was praised for the way in which he refused to feel sorry for himself and carried on as normally as he was able. People also admired Marion for her devotion to him. He engaged in energetic research about Parkinson's disease and campaigned for a revolutionary new treatment. This was based on the implanting of part of a foetus into the brain. It was to be offered on the National Health Service. When the process was finally available in 1991, Jeremy was treated – but it had little effect. Yet this failure did not deter him. From the time his illness became known in the mid-1980s, Jeremy was willing to try anything that might improve his health. Determined to maintain his social life he attended dinners, parties and memorial services until his illness made it difficult for him to eat without help.

By that time too, Marion's family had developed their own careers. Her eldest son David was a film and television producer. Her youngest son Jeremy was a successful business executive in the music industry, at that time working with Richard Branson at Virgin. James, a musician, had married a second time and was living in New Mexico with his wife and two children There were a growing number of grandchildren ranging from babies to teenagers. Marion did her best to see as much as possible of them. James greatly missed his mother but over the next ten years he came over with his children five or six times. Despite Jeremy's growing incapacity from Parkinson's, he and Marion could still travel and went out to the US to see James.

A medicine man living in the community of which James and his family were members thought he could help Jeremy with herbal remedies. And so did a Nigerian doctor living in Arizona. This doctor had a father who practised herbal medicine in Nigeria and James told his mother and Jeremy that they should come over. Marion was as keen as her husband. and James remembers a huge concoction of herbs being plunged into Jeremy's posterior which helped a lot for a while. Jeremy also took part in a ceremony on James's property in which he was put in a sweat lodge where the porous volcanic rocks of New Mexico were heated. Jeremy looked about five years younger when he emerged, said James. The remedies, although helpful, were difficult to sustain in the UK and sadly the illness continued to develop.

Marion had adopted the cottage at Higher Chuggaton in Devon as a valued retreat for the family and until Jeremy's reduced mobility made visits to the cottage impossible, the couple spent much time there. For some years Marion was president of the South West Arts Association. During that time, the association celebrated its 25th anniversary and an event known as 'President's Choice' was organised to mark the occasion. Marion chose the parish church at South Molton and invited her friends Slava Rostropovich and Yehudi Menuhin to play. The church was packed. Reflecting in his memoirs about his wife's role in the Association at that time, Jeremy paid her a moving tribute. "She brings to this (her presidency) as to everything else that she touches, a calm, imaginative and wise counsel. For my part no man could have a more perfect companion."[99] As Jeremy's health deteriorated, living in the cottage became ever more problematical. With its narrow passages and stairs and uneven surfaces, it became extremely hazardous for him. But it remained a much-loved retreat, one which Rupert in particular considered home. Marion's many grandchildren were welcomed there. But inevitably, as Jeremy's health worsened, the convenience of living in London became increasingly more practical.

But that was much later and there were good times

in Devon before then. As the trial faded into memory, Jeremy became more acceptable to his old Liberal party and in March 1987 was elected President of the North Devon Liberals. He and Marion campaigned together for the Liberal candidate who was hoping to secure Jeremy's old parliamentary seat. Partly thanks to their enthusiastic support, the Liberal candidate halved the Conservative majority. A few years later, in 1992 Jeremy and Marion supported Nick Harvey who won back the seat for the Liberal Democrats, the new party recently formed from the merger of the Liberals with the Social Democrats. Jeremy was enjoying being 'in the loop' again and hearing the news from Westminster. Marion supported him in his revived interest in his old party.

In November 1994 an interesting case involving the Liberal Democrats was brought before Mr Justice Dyson (now Lord Dyson)[100] and Mr Justice Forbes in the Election Court. Earlier that year, the Devon and East Plymouth European Parliament seat had been contested by a man called Richard Huggett, calling himself a **Literal** Democrat. Over 10,000 people had voted for him and the Conservative candidate, Giles Chichester, won the seat from the Liberal Democrats by a mere 700 votes. The Liberal candidate Adrian Sanders complained to the Election Court that 10,000 people had probably voted in error, thinking they were voting for his party. He claimed that he already had 505 signatures to say they had voted in error and he asked for a re-run of the election. However, despite in their written judgement accepting that people might well have been confused, the judges ruled against Mr Sanders. According to the law at that time, Richard

Huggett had been validly nominated. Jeremy, as a lawyer, was interested in the case and went to court to observe the proceedings. Lord Dyson remembers that just before the start of the case, Marion helped her husband into the back of the courtroom where both stayed, listening intently as the action proceeded.

Slowly, the couple began to be more visibly involved in the life of the Party. When the Lib Dems gained forty-six seats at the General Election of 1997, Marion and Jeremy hosted a reception at Orme Square for the West Country MPs. Jeremy made an amusing speech saying that the party now had John O'Groats and Land's End and all they had to do now was fill in the spaces between. That year he and Marion went to the party conference for the first time since the trial, 18 years before. He was welcomed enthusiastically by the delegates although the leadership were less enthusiastic. His need to be visible was rewarded by interest from the Press, interest that, as usual, Jeremy welcomed.

Another of his interests was his dream of a peerage. He researched a possible claim to a medieval peerage associated with his family. This came to nothing. Unashamedly he talked to everyone he knew who might be able to sway his old party into recommending him for a peerage as a reward for his past achievements. But it never happened. He had not been forgiven sufficiently for his party to support him and, as people pointed out, he was no longer able to make an audible speech.

EIGHTEEN

The 1990s -
A Changing Family

Marion loved her family which was still growing and becoming more dispersed. She sometimes found it difficult to accept immediately the changed relationships of her sons. Her eldest son David recalled that when he left his wife in 1990 for Diane, now his Countess, Marion seemed disapproving at first. Intensely loyal herself, she might have seen this as a repeat of what had happened in her own first marriage. However, she soon accepted her new daughter-in-law and Diane recalls how interested Marion was in her career as an artist. On one occasion, Diane had an exhibition in a London art gallery and Marion came to the opening. Diane was not sure how her always elegantly dressed mother-in-law would fit in with the motley assortment of other visitors, and kept an eye on her. Realising that she was missing from the room, as were many people who should have been viewing the paintings, Diane, worried, searched for her. She found that Marion had been 'adopted' by a couple of gay men and was installed on a chair outside the gallery, smoking, and entertaining a small crowd. Marion always attracted people to her.

James too had married again; to Joy, in the late 1990s. Marion had known Joy since she was a young girl in the late 1960s when Marion's two younger sons James and Jeremy had just left 'Westminster School and were starting their first band. Joy and the boys had mutual friends and they all went to hear bands together. When Joy visited James at Orme Square "of course she had to meet Marion." In the garden as she remembers. As long as she knew her, says Joy, Marion was not far behind where her boys were. Joy was a guest at James' first marriage in 1973 but lost contact when James left for America and a new life there. Years later, in the mid 1990s and after a difficult second divorce, James returned to England and moved in with Marion and Jeremy, living in the flat at the top of the house in Orme Square. He and Joy met again when he found her address and contacted her. When they decided to marry, they both lived in the flat together. Marion could not leave Jeremy to go to either of their two weddings, one in Nigeria with Joy's family and another on the Island of Anguilla where George and Patricia had a winter home. But she celebrated with the young couple at Orme Square before they left for their honeymoon and invited Joy's sisters who lived in London to the party. James' divorce had been acrimonious and Joy found the constant communication from his ex-wife very difficult. Joy remembers Marion as a friend and confidante with whom she could share her concerns. She appreciated too the interest that Marion had in Joy's family. It was very welcome she says to people who have moved from their country of birth. Marion took Joy's London family in, inviting her sisters to dinner and enjoying the company of their children in the holidays.

Marion's nature was one which included other people without judgement of them. She was a good listener but wary about expressing her opinions. Although she had been strongly affected by the end of her own first marriage and its early aftermath and had reacted strongly against people then who did not take her side, things had changed. Perhaps, as a result of that early upset, she worked to keep her extended family together, even after marriages had ended. She liked her early daughters-in-law as well as the current ones and made sure that everyone was invited to family events. Rupert remembers what he calls 'an ex-wives club' of which Marion was the pack leader.

As Jeremy's health deteriorated the couple spent as much time as possible in Devon where Jeremy could enjoy his garden and Marion could enjoy the company of invited friends. Although there was a grand piano at the cottage as well as the London Steinway, and although music was always to be heard wherever Marion was, she did not play for friends or for her own pleasure. One day at the cottage however, remains fixed in the memory of her friend Iona Salinger. Iona was staying with Marion along with Winifred (Win) Roberts, an Australian born violinist who Marion had known since they studied together at the Royal College of Music. She and Marion had given recitals together as young professional musicians. Now in the late 1990s, Win, the newly bereaved widow of harpsichordist Geraint Jones, was a welcome visitor to Devon. Marion was somehow persuaded to play with Win and the three women laughed at the occasional odd notes, enjoying the rare experience. Perhaps Jeremy heard it too. His hearing was acute even as his other faculties began to shut down and he became increasingly dependent on Marion's care. By this time, Marion herself was beginning to need help herself. She had arthritis. However, she insisted on caring for Jeremy herself.

Jeremy was still as active as it was possible to be. Although he was failing physically due to his disease, his mind was still sharp. Publicity about his life, although much of it detrimental, seemed to enthuse him; he revelled in such interest in his past. In autumn 1996 *Rinkagate* was published, an account of how the *Pencourt File* [101] came to be written which contained Norman's Scott's view of Jeremy. One of its authors, Barrie Penrose, half of the Pencourt duo who had researched the Thorpe affair, recalled a visit to see Jeremy in 1995. He had phoned the number given but thought the whisper that he heard was a fault in the telephone line. Ringing again he got Marion's firm assertive voice. She explained that Jeremy was not well and distrusted reporters but when Penrose asked if he could drop in and pay his respects, she said he might. Calling at the cottage in the summer heat, he was met by Marion dressed in an old frock and sandals. Although Jeremy was not available, a meeting was fixed for the following day at 11. Promptly at the appointed hour, Penrose knocked and Marion, dressed formally, opened the door and ushered Penrose into a sunny room overlooking the garden and offered coffee. Jeremy was a sad figure, very thin and struggling to speak. Although he said a lot, it was little more than a mixture of bluster about journalists, and threats. Marion calmly interpreted. But it was not a successful interview. Thorpe said he was going to write his autobiography and did not want to 'scoop' himself. Marion, realising that her husband was tired of talking, offered to show Penrose the converted barn. Thorpe led the way and gave a guided tour which was impossible to understand. It was a beautiful room but like a mausoleum Penrose recalled, full of photographs and mementoes of Jeremy's political past, his election victories. There was also a magnificent piano which Marion explained she rarely played these days. The journalist realised that he was not going to get any new explanations from Thorpe and was very glad to leave the house.

Interest in what happened almost twenty years previously, continued intermittently. A BBC television documentary *Secret Lives – Jeremy Thorpe,* also in 1996, pulled no punches as most of the players in the Norman Scott drama told their tales. Perhaps such adverse publicity spurred Jeremy on to consider his own book of reminiscences, his autobiography. In the following two years, punctuated by a 1998 silver wedding celebration at which Moura Lympany, (the pianist who had introduced Marion and Jeremy) played, he worked on his new project. Marion and his devoted secretary Judy Young helped him collect and collate his memoirs and in 1999, *In My Own Time* was published. Unfortunately, the book is not a coherent memoir and readers did not find anything new about Jeremy as a man. It is a loose collection of what Jeremy considered his political successes, family and home details and odd stories. There were a few heavier chapters, such as a submission to a commission on electoral reform that he had then recently proposed. His publisher Ian Dale who had recently set up Politico publishing tried to get him to write more fully about his trial, but Jeremy would not consider it. The reviews were honest about the paucity of real content but kind in recalling Jeremy's flair as a political performer.

But as ever fully supportive, Marion was happy to help her husband succeed in his ventures. They threw a huge reception at the National Liberal Club to launch the book, one filled with friends and colleagues from the past. Despite real problems in speaking, he made a speech which was difficult to hear but which those near enough to him said was amusing and lively. His son Rupert came over from America and his stepsons, David, James and Jeremy loyally attended. "Ensconced in the centre of the room, frail but alert, the handsome figure of Marion standing protectively by his side, he drew his guests towards him with a certain magnetism."[102]

Early in the 1990s Jeremy had agreed to cooperate in a biography written by Michael Bloch. The author remembers meeting Marion and Jeremy for the first time at Orme Square in April 1993, just before Jeremy's sixty-fourth birthday. He was, Bloch remembers, a sick man but "his mind was still active and his will to live manifest." Marion was very protective towards him. Bloch was treated with courtesy by them both, but they were wary. Jeremy would not talk about his trial and his homosexuality and Bloch never managed to lift what he called the shutters that came down whenever he broached the subjects. The couple felt strongly that the book should not come out until after Jeremy's death, and it was thought that, given

Jeremy's condition, the biography was most likely to be posthumous. In the event, Jeremy lasted longer than most people with Parkinson's; his determination to take part in normal life sustained him. In 1993 he was losing the ability to walk without falling but by 1994, through sheer determination, he was able to do so again. He insisted on speaking and telling stories even when he could barely be heard. He lived with the condition for thirty-five years. Publication was indeed posthumous. It was 16th December 2014, 10 days after the death of its subject that the hardback first edition of the biography came out. Marion, who died just six months before her husband, never lived to read it.

By the 1990s when the biography was being discussed, Marion had resigned from some of her many positions. due to the need to care for her husband. Although she had resigned from her role as vice-chairman of the Leeds Piano Competition in 1983, Marion still maintained her links with Leeds, with the competition and with Fanny Waterman. In 2000, she hosted an eightieth birthday party for Fanny at her home. It was a small gathering of about twenty people with guests including musical friends, Janet Baker and Lady Solti. Lord John Dyson, then a High Court Judge, later to become Master of the Rolls, was also invited. Originally from Leeds, he had been a pupil of Fanny Waterman in the 1950s – his lesson on a Sunday morning, he remembers, was sandwiched between those of Allan Schiller and of Michael Roll, both of which went on to have careers as concert pianists. Jeremy, by then in a wheelchair entered the room and Marion beckoned John to sit beside her husband and talk to him. By this time, Jeremy could not speak although his hearing was still acute. Although one-sided, with Lord Dyson speaking and Jeremy indicating his interest without speaking, the two managed to communicate about the Liberal cause and especially about the Literal Democrat case which Jeremy had witnessed some six years earlier. Lord Dyson remembers how solicitous Marion was about her husband's welfare and how she wanted him to be included in the party.

In the early 2000s there was plenty of family in Orme Square. The house had lots of room. James and his wife Joy had moved into the self-contained cottage in the back garden which had probably once been for a housekeeper. James's daughter Sophie and her partner came to live in the flat upstairs in the house. In 2010 Lilianda, Sophie's daughter was born, a baby great-granddaughter for Marion. Having the house full of people brought back family life to the chilly old house, a very welcome support to Marion in her later years. Although the units were separate, family members were able to see Marion regularly and had supper with her in the evenings when they could. There were family get-togethers which Marion enjoyed. Rupert remembers her in her eighties playing the adult version of the board game Guess Who, a game in which players are required to ask questions about the characters' 'more sensitive parts of the anatomy'. She thought it funny and enjoyed it hugely.

In 2001, as intrepid as ever, Marion and Jeremy flew to Los Angeles for the wedding of Rupert, now a successful photographer, and his wife Caroline. Their return journey was on '9/11', the date of the terrible attack on the Twin Tower building in New York. Flights were grounded and they were marooned for some days. In 2005, David, Marion's eldest son accompanied her to Vienna to a celebration of her father Erwin, as one of Schonberg's pupils and friends. The celebration included the launch of a book about Erwin, one of a series about Schonberg's associates. While in Vienna, Marion said, people looked at her strangely when she spoke to them. Of course, her Austrian German, although correct, was what she had heard as a girl in the 1930s. David said that it would have been like someone who spoke the clipped English of actress Celia Johnson, the star of the film 'Brief Encounter' trying to communicate with people in England now. It was Marion's last visit to Vienna, the city of her birth, from where, as an apprehensive young refugee, she had left in 1938.

She was extremely loyal to Jeremy, sometimes to her detriment. Eventually his demands exhausted her. Whilst he remained in command of his faculties, he was attentive and interested in his step family; more so than George, who was very reserved, remembers James. He particularly enjoyed being a step-grandfather. However, as his faculties, (except for his hearing which remained acute), closed-down, he was more difficult to get on with. His medication caused him to suffer upsetting delusions. It was harder for him to be part of social occasions. Iona Salinger was delegated to sit by him sometimes at dinner as she had acute hearing and so could communicate with Jeremy. Although they employed carers, Jeremy wanted Marion to look after him, not realising that she could not help as she used to do. Sometimes he drove her to distraction with his demands. By the early 2000s, Marion, not well herself, was caring for Jeremy, supported by family members and

Lilia, in the house at Orme Square. It was not an easy house for Jeremy to navigate in his wheel chair. The house was becoming slightly shabby and inconvenient. They began to need more help to live there in comfort, and extra carers were employed to help.

In 2007 eighty-one-year-old Marion had a major stroke which robbed her of mobility and speech. Although physically needing a wheelchair to get around, she determinedly worked hard at her speech and soon began to talk again. Physically exercising was a different matter and she had to be persuaded to do short walks to regain a little mobility. Not being able to do it right frustrated her. Although they were both in wheelchairs, Marion and Jeremy insisted on staying in their loved but inconvenient home and had a lift installed so that they could move from floor to floor in their wheelchairs in the big old house. In 2009 Jeremy celebrated his 80th birthday. He had now outlived many of his contemporaries and his past successes were remembered rather than his fall from grace. He was now coming to be regarded as the 'grand old man' of his Party. In true Jeremy style, he threw a birthday party for 150 in the smoking room at the National Liberal Club. He made a witty speech although only those close by could hear him. One of his guests recalled, "The champagne flowed all evening and I can see them both now, in separate wheelchairs but 'parked' close together, holding hands and smiling."[103]

A few days after his party, a bust of him that had been prepared when he was leader of the party almost fifty years earlier, but then put aside, was finally unveiled in the Grimond Room of the House of Commons by the speaker, John Bercow. This was to be Jeremy's last public appearance. He spent his final years quietly, reminiscing about the past and seeing family and friends. Marion still went up to Harewood to see her family there. David remembers one quiet lunch in 2011 at home with just his wife Diane, his father George, Patricia, and his mother. It was a happy day. George and Marion shared memories of their time together and the people and places that they had known. George died just a few days later.

Right to the end, Marion was still interested in what was going on outside of London and her home. She never lost her zest for new experience. She had two late holidays abroad, to Tenerife and to Marrakesh, accompanied by a helper, James and his wife, his daughter Sophie and her daughter Lilianda. Sadly, although she loved opera, she refused to go to performances at Covent Garden in her wheelchair. If the glamour of the Crush Bar and opera house receptions were beyond her participation, she preferred not to go. However, she was still remembered for her place in musical history and still considered someone worthy of listening to on musical matters. She had not been forgotten. On October 3, 2003, fifty years after the death of Kathleen Ferrier, the BBC aired a television programme about the singer's life, *An Ordinary Diva*. Marion, seated for the filming in her Orme Square drawing room, smartly dressed in a skirt, white blouse and beige jacket, reminisced about the friend of so long ago. She remembered the fun and Kathleen's Passing Cloud brand cigarettes. She told viewers that Britten had first heard Kathleen when she sang in a National Gallery Concert during the war at a time when Marion lived in

Britten's house. Presumably the extended family discussed this exciting new singer that night. Ben had written *The Rape of Lucretia* for Kathleen and Marion remembered them both working intensively in the lovely surroundings of Glyndebourne. The opera premiered there 12 July 1946. It was a challenge for Glyndebourne to reopen after the war with a new opera, said Marion.

Even though now wheelchair bound since her stroke, Marion remained an active contributor to many musical causes until her caring role for Jeremy took too much of her time and her own health began to fail. In 2013, as part of the celebrations of the centenary of Britten's birth, Marion, then 86, was interviewed by Tom Service on BBC radio 3. The programme, *Marion Thorpe and Benjamin Britten: An Intimate Friendship* covered the long period during which Marion had known the composer, from being introduced to him by her father in 1939 to the composer's death in 1976. She remembered being familiar at an early stage with all the operas and main musical pieces that were composed when her family lived with Britten and Pears. She treated Ben with respect as a great composer as well as a friend, but she must have done something right, she said. Unlike the many people he discarded because they tried to get too close or he felt were using him in some way, she was always in favour. Only on the tennis court was she unpopular. Ben was a good tennis player and Marion was not. He loved to win and was not pleased when at tennis parties on the courts at the Red House, he had to partner her in mixed doubles and they would most often lose. "He didn't like it at all," said Marion.

When Diane visited Marion in hospital shortly before

she died in 2014, she was listening to her music and reading classical novels again. Typically, instead of complaining about her own situation, she wanted to talk about what Diane, an artist, was doing.

But perhaps the most important recognition of her contribution to the arts in Britain had come a few years earlier. In 2008, as a summary to her musical life and as a reward for her achievements she was awarded the CBE[104] in Queen Elizabeth II's birthday honours for services to music, particularly for her role in starting the iconic Leeds International Piano Competition. The same birthday honours gave her friend Fanny Waterman, with who she began the competition, a Damehood. Marion was immensely proud of her CBE. Typical of her loyalty, she almost refused the honour as she felt that it was Jeremy who should receive an honour, not her. But at heart she knew that the peerage he sought so long would never happen, and she accepted her own award.

Epilogue

So, who was Marion?

Her life was one of many contrasts: from a schoolgirl refugee to a countess married to royalty, from a schoolgirl to a concert pianist, from being the wife of a successful politician to coping with scandal and his rejection. It was from being a mother of grown sons to a mother of a small son again, from an unwanted divorce to a marriage of many highs and lows. Although there were times when she led what was to many an enviable lifestyle, life was not always easy for Marion. She endured more than her fair share of vicissitudes, none of her own making and all because of her relationships with the men in her life: her father and both her husbands. As a Jew, her adored father had moved his family away from their comfortable home to an unknown future. She had married two strong men. Marion married George Lascelles for love and was devastated when her love was not enough for him and he chose someone else. She married Jeremy Thorpe and by all accounts this developed into a mutually loving relationship although she made a lot of sacrifices for him. Living with both husbands provided many good times but in neither of her marriages had things turned out as Marion had expected when she married. Whether she ever regretted any of the choices she had made in life, she never admitted them. She firmly believed in the old adage, 'as you make your bed so you must lie on it'. She had, however, a large and supportive family from her time as Countess of Harewood and gained a new family from her youngest son, Rupert, whom she had mothered from the time he was a very small child.

Her life as a countess which lasted for eighteen years before it ended, contained less than ten years of happiness. And her anticipated life as the wife of a successful politician did not last very long. There is no doubt that she cared for both of her husbands a great deal and, for different reasons, was determined that each marriage would succeed. She was immensely loyal and was perhaps more upset than most people would be when that loyalty was not reciprocated and her first marriage deteriorated. She was loyal beyond what could ever have been expected to her second husband. Jeremy Thorpe's son Rupert feels that although his parents' marriage might have seemed strange to outsiders, the couple came together at the right time for both and that the combination worked. He felt his father only lasted as long as he did due to Marion's support. The obituary of Marion in the Independent newspaper also emphasised her importance to Thorpe in a moving tribute to their marriage. "Her great gift to Thorpe over the turbulent years that followed, through his fall from public life, and his three decades darkened by illness, was her loyalty. No matter what might be said by those who opposed him, posterity must surely record that it says something for the quality of a man that he had such a wife."[105]

A friend's reflection on Marion's character sums it up. "Marion was, as I suppose all of us are, pretty complicated and an elusive character." Although she could be regal and had a reputation for coldness, especially when she felt intrusion, this seems to have been a reserve she used only when needed. In public, despite what she might have strongly felt in private, she was inclined to sit on the fence about issues and leave comment to others. This reserve may well have been due to the ups and downs in her life, the uncertainties she had weathered. She had such a difficult life and had seen hopes turn into failure. To all those who knew her well however, she was seen as a warm, affectionate, and above all a loyal person. She maintained friendships over many years and those friends loved her and felt comfortable in her company. When Jeremy died, her stepson Rupert wrote to say how devotedly Marion had raised him, as well as standing by his father 'through everything'. She was very stoic, Rupert remembered, "but she had a lot to put up with." David, her eldest son recalled that all her many grandchildren and great grandchildren adored her. She was funny and retained a wicked and ribald sense of humour.

Music sustained her throughout her life. It was always part of her, and when defining herself outside marriage it was as a musician. Although she gave up music as a profession when she first married, she made a great contribution to music in Britain from an early age. She facilitated the appearances of many 20th century musicians in the country and befriended modern composers including Benjamin Britten. She was involved in the careers of young pianists by providing a showcase for the best young talent at the Leeds International Piano Competition that she co-founded and often contacted influential friends to request that they book young musicians to play. She also encouraged piano learners, young and old, with her piano primers. Invitations to speak on music matters on the BBC recognised her knowledge and influence and she was appointed to a plethora of roles in musical organisations. The award of the MBE for her services to music in 2008 was a fitting recognition.

She was always a party-girl remembers one of her friends, Iona Salinger. She loved having lots of people around her, the chance to dress up, new experiences. She was, of course Viennese and, to misquote the proverb, you could take the girl out of Vienna but not Vienna out of the girl. Perhaps in Marion's readiness to use her home to facilitate concerts, parties, recitals and meetings and to bring together many people from different walks of life, she was unconsciously recreating the salons of Enlightenment Vienna which her forbears would have known.

She also liked the company of young people. She encouraged their musical and artistic aspirations both formally in the world of classical music and much more informally as she supported her sons' band and their lifestyle; a lifestyle completely different to her own. Looking back on the late 1960s and early 1970s when Marion's Orme Square house sometimes rocked with pop music, George Stedman, a friend of Marion's sons, posted this heartfelt tribute on Facebook when she died.

"A truly exceptional lady who influenced all our lives through her generosity of spirit. She came from a world of glittering concert halls, surrounded by famous classical musicians, composers, royalty and political leaders, but she still had time for a band of scruffy dropouts (us!) who she allowed to invade her exclusive residence. She was no stranger to intrigue and scandal, but always blameless herself and fiercely loyal to her own. She loved no-one more than her own sons, David, James and Jeremy, and if you were a friend of theirs, you were a friend of hers and she would do anything for you.

It was a privilege to have known her and to have that glimpse of a world of grandeur, great art, power and fame that she inhabited."[106]

That life of grandeur and fame had not lasted but she faced the difficult things in her life with an outward calm and essentially pragmatic approach. She packed into two thirds of her lifetime, more experiences, both good and bad, than most people could come up against in many lifetimes. She had been a visible public figure. The last part of her life was mostly played well out of the public gaze. She never had the calm widowhood that those who knew her probably expected and maybe hoped for, pre-deceasing her ailing husband by six months.

As she grew older, she continued to pay attention to what was happening around her. She was interested still in politics and music, the varied lives of her sons and her grandchildren. The things that had offered her pleasure in the past, she continued to embrace with enthusiasm. She enjoyed new things in her life. One day, after being pushed around the park in her wheelchair she remarked on how, for the first time, she had really looked up with interest at the trees above her, something, she said, she could never have done when walking. She enjoyed the company of friends and family and despite her disability still remembered the fun of her life when young.

One evening late in her life, she was up at Harewood to celebrate the wedding of her grandson Ben. By then both she and her first husband George were confined to wheelchairs. When George was leaving to go to bed, he asked to be pushed over to say goodnight to Marion.

"Oh George," she said, smiling at him, "I thought we were going to dance."

Acknowledgements

In writing this book about Marion Stein, later Lascelles and Thorpe, I am indebted to many people, but perhaps primarily to her eldest son, David Lascelles, 8th Earl of Harewood and his wife Diane. They allowed my access to the many letters, papers and photographs in the archive store at Harewood House. Their kindness and hospitality made the research for this book a real pleasure.

Other members of the Lascelles family too, Marion's sons James and Jeremy, daughter-in-law Joy, and granddaughters Sophie and Tanit, were willing to give generously of their time to talk to me about Marion as a mother, mother-in-law and grandmother. Molly Kelly, the butler at Harewood was able to tell me about Marion's visits to Harewood in later life.

Rupert Thorpe, Marion's stepson gave me wonderful insights into how Marion and his father Jeremy created secure family homes for him in both London and Devon, despite the pressures on the couple when he was young.

Research into Marion's connections with Benjamin Britten and Aldeburgh required me to access the significant Britten Pears archive at the Red House in Suffolk. Dr Nick Clark and his colleague provided a collection of many papers, letters and photographs relating to both Marion's and her parent's relationships with Benjamin Britten. Dr Clark and Colin Matthews were able to give me their personal recollections of Marion's continued work with Aldeburgh and the Red House after Britten's death.

Many people who had known Marion in some way during her long life were willing to share their reminiscences. Talks with Iona Salinger, a London friend since the 1970s gave insights into Marion's character and how she coped with the ups and downs in her life during her second marriage. Michael Roll, the Leeds born concert pianist remembered clearly the first Leeds International Piano Competition in 1963 when he won the first prize. His anecdotes of the competition and of Marion's role in it, were invaluable to the story. Lord John Dyson, a Leeds-born judge and ex Master of the Rolls recounted anecdotes both from his time in Leeds when young and from his meetings with Marion and Jeremy Thorpe later in his life. Nigel Jackson, once vicar of Swimbridge in Devon recalled for me incidents of Marion's life in her Devon home.

There were other people, Stephanie Rolt at the Royal Opera House, Helen Skilbeck at Leeds Central Library and Alex Pearson, Archive assistant W Yorkshire Archive service who were able to point me to useful sources of information for the book. Biddy Hayward, Nick Clarke, Philippa Taylor and especially Lauren Fowler have helped to source and organise the illustrations. A chance hearing on Radio 3 of Helena Newman, Chairman of Sotheby's Europe, speaking about her life, led to an email conversation and to the reading of her father's book, a wonderful evocation of teenage life in 1938 Vienna and provided an unexpected link between her father and Erwin Stein.

And to all those at my publisher Troubador who have brought this book to fruition, thank you.

Perhaps a good example of the serendipity that makes research so interesting and enjoyable happened at Thorpeness, near Aldeburgh when I was nearing the end of my writing. On a hot August day, incidentally my birthday, after finishing some research in the Britten-Pears archive, we decided to search for Marion's seaside house at Thorpeness. Quite unexpectedly we met Michael and Marianne Shorrock, the current owners. My birthday was spent being shown the house, sitting in glorious sunshine in a room overlooking the sea and enjoying talking to two of the most hospitable people about Marion.

So, my heartfelt thanks go to everyone who made this book possible; those who willingly contributed and to the many whose writings and broadcasts have added so much to the book but whom I will probably never meet. I hoped that I have referenced them all.

And not least, my love and appreciation go to my partner Keith Alldritt. He has helped the research, provided his literary expertise, and has encouraged me all the way.

References

1   George Newman, Finding Harmony. Publisher George Newman 2013. Kindle edition loc. 887

2   Quote by John Amis in The three lives of Marion Thorpe, Stephen Pollard, June 7, 2018 https://www.thejc.com/news/features/the-three-lives-of-marion-thorpe-jeremy-thorpe-a-very-english-scandal-1.465267 in https://www.thejc.com/news/features/the-three-lives-of-marion-thorpe-jeremy-thorpe-a-very-english-scandal-1.465267

3   Letters from a Life, Volume 1 The Selected Letters and Diaries of Benjamin Britten. Editor Donald Mitchell. Faber and Faber 1991 P 127

4   Ibid P 354

5   Ibid P 354

6   George Newman, Finding Harmony. Publisher George Newman 2013 Kindle edition loc. 5549

7   Sir Thomas Beecham, 1979-1961, English Conductor and impresario.

8   8-3-43 Letter 413 p1117

9   Benjamin Britten-A Life for Music. Neil Powell, Windmill Books 2013 p248

10 Benjamin Britten, A Life in the Twentieth Century, Paul Kildea, Allen Lane 2013, p258

11 Letters from a Life. Vol 3 Benjamin Britten(1946-51) 8/8/47, P103

12 Benjamin Britten had written an operetta Paul Bunyan (1941) while in the US

13 Quote from Marion's recollections of her life in family archive.

14 John Amis, (1922-2013) British broadcaster, classical music critic, music administrator and writer.

15 Benjamin Britten, A Biography, Humphrey Carpenter, Faber and Faber Ltd. 1992 P233

16 Benjamin Britten, A Life in the Twentieth Century, Paul Kildea, Allen Lane 2013, p278

17 Benjamin Britten, A Life in the Twentieth Century, Paul Kildea, Allen Lane 2013, p258

18 Eric Crozier (his and Nancy Evans' autobiography After Long Pursuit

19 Quote from Marion's recollections of her life in family archive.

20 Letters from a Life. Vol 3 Benjamin Britten(1946-51) 8/8/47, P306

21 The Tongs and Bones, Lord Harewood, 1981, Weidenfeld and Nicholson P86-87

22 Ibid P 101

23 Letters from a Life. Vol 3 Benjamin Britten (1946-51) P473

24 The Tongs and Bones, Lord Harewood, 1981, Weidenfeld and Nicholson. P103

25 Quote from Marion's recollections of her life in family archive

26 Letters from a Life. Vol 3 Benjamin Britten (1946-51) P 507

27 YouTube coverage of Lord Harewood's engagement, Pathe and Movietone 25 July 1949

28 The Tongs and Bones, Lord Harewood, 1981, Weidenfeld and Nicholson P103

29 Harewood, The Life and Times of an English Country House, Hutchinson 1982. P140

30 Ibid P140

31 Liberal History News, Spring 2014. Ronald Porter

32 Essential Britten: John Bridcut. Faber and Faber 2013. Kindle edition P23

33 Ibid P159

34 London Remembers https://www.londonremembers.com

35 Princess Mary, The First Modern Princess. Elizabeth Basford. The History press, 2021 P

36 Ibid P103

37 Ibid P 204

38 The Tongs and Bones, Lord Harewood, 1981, Weidenfeld and Nicholson P 97

39 Post by Marlene Eilers Koenig at Tuesday, July 12, 2011

40 The Tongs and Bones, Lord Harewood, 1981, Weidenfeld and Nicholson P119

41 Letters from a Life. Vol 3 Benjamin Britten (1946-51) Letter 25 March 1950. P584-5 Letter 659

42 Ibid P620 Letter 680

43 Ibid P623 Letter 682

44 Kathleen: The Life of Kathleen Ferrier Maurice Leonard. The History Press. E book 2012. Location 3233

45 Benjamin Britten – A Biography. Humphrey Carpenter, Faber and Faber 1992

46 Peter Pears – a Biography. Christopher Headington, Faber and Faber 1991 P166.

47 The Tongs and Bones, Lord Harewood, 1981, Weidenfeld and Nicholson P107

48 The Tongs and Bones, Lord Harewood, 1981, Weidenfeld and Nicholson P108

49 The Tongs and Bones, Lord Harewood, 1981, Weidenfeld and Nicholson P106

50 Letters from a Life. Vol 5, 1958-1965 Benjamin Britten. Boydell Press 2010 footnote 9, P103

51 Benjamin Britten, A Life in the Twentieth Century, Paul Kildea, Allen Lane 2013, p439

52 Ibid P99

53 Russian Empire-born composer and conductor who lived and worked in Paris and became a citizen of both France and Italy.

54 Benjamin Britten-A Life for Music. Neil Powell, Windmill Books 2013 P

55 In My Own Time, Jeremy Thorpe. Politico's Publishing 1999

56 A Hare Marked Moon, David Lascelles. Unbound 2021 P21

57 Pursuit. The Uncensored Memoirs of John Calder, John Calder, Calder Publications, London 2001. P269

58 Letters from a Life. Vol 5, 1958-1965 Benjamin Britten. Boydell Press 2010 P630

59 Letters in Harewood archive.

60 The Tongs and Bones, Lord Harewood, 1981, Weidenfeld and Nicholson P295

61 The Tongs and Bones, Lord Harewood, 1981, Weidenfeld and Nicholson P220

62 Covent Garden – the Untold Story, Norman Lebrecht, Simon and Schuster UK ltd 2000 p279

63 Letters from a Life. Vol 5, 1958-1965 Benjamin Britten. Boydell Press 2010 P161

64 Ibid P211 (footnote 5)

65 Ibid P223

66 Letters from a Life. Vol 5, 1958-1965 Benjamin Britten. Boydell Press P712

67 Daily Express. 2 January 1966

68 Covent Garden – the Untold Story, Norman Lebrecht, Simon and Schuster UK ltd 2000 P228

69 Jack Lyons was a Leeds businessman, financier and philanthropist. he was charged in 1987 in the Guiness share trading fraud He was convicted and was heavily fined. Lyons had been awarded the CBE in 1967 and knighted

in 1973 for public and charitable services and services to the arts, but both these honours were rescinded in 1991 in the wake of his conviction.

70 Piano Competition: The Story of the Leeds. Wendy Thompson with Fanny Waterman, Faber and Faber, London 1991

71 The Cold War. 1947-1991. A period of geopolitical tension between the the United States and the Soviet Union and their respective allies. 1

72 The Profumo Affair was a major political scandal. John Profumo the Secretary of State for War in Harold McMillan's Conservative Government had an affair with Christine Keeler, a nineteen- year-old model beginning in 1961. Profumo lied about it to the Commons and the scandal was a contributor to McMillan;s resignation in 1963 and the defeat of the Conservatives by the Labour party in the 1964 general election.

73 Youtube interview, Lord Dyson of Fanny Waterman. 3 May 2018, Leeds University. Dame Fanny Waterman – A Life in Music.

74 James Blades OBE (9 September 1901 – 19 May 1999) was an English percussionist. One of the most distinguished percussionists in Western music. His book *Percussion Instruments and their History* (1971) is a standard reference work on the subject. He was a long-time associate of Benjamin Britten with whom he conceived many of the composer's unusual percussion effects.

75 1936 British documentary film directed and produced by Harry Watt and Basil Wright, produced by the General Post Office (GPO) Film Unit.

76 Edward Heath – The Course of my Life. Autobiography. Hodder and Stoughton. 1998

77 Jeremy Thorpe Michael Bloch, Abacus Books, 2014. Kindle edition Location 2599

78 Funeral oration for Jeremy Thorpe by Nick Harvey 2014. Liberal Democrats Tiverton and Honiton. tivandhonlibdems.org.uk

79 Diary of Lord Beaumont 7 June 1968. Quoted in Jeremy Thorpe Michael Bloch, Abacus Books, 2014. Kindle edition Location 4233

80 Jeremy Thorpe Michael Bloch, Abacus Books, 2014. Kindle edition Location 4680

81 The Three Lives of Marion Thorpe. Jewish Chronicle 7 June 2018

82 Ibid. Location 2196Quoting from P Bessell, Cover-Up, the Jeremy Thorpe Affair, Wilmington Simons Books, 1980

83 Closet Queens, Michael Bloch, Little. Brown 2015. Kindle version Location 3604

84 A Very English Scandal, John Preston, Penguin 2016 P 165

85 Facebook tribute to Marion by George, one of the Globs band. 8 March 2014

86 Jeremy Thorpe Michael Bloch, Abacus Books, 2014. Kindle edition Location 5240

87 Jeremy Thorpe Michael Bloch, Abacus Books, 2014. Kindle edition Location 5188

88 Jeremy Thorpe Michael Bloch, Abacus Books, 2014. (Quoted as information from Lord Banks, 1918-1997, Liberal Peer.) Kindle edition Location 5284

89 Jeremy Thorpe Michael Bloch, Abacus Books , 2014. Kindle edition Location 6115

90 A Very English Scandal, John Preston, Penguin 2016 P225

91 Ibid Location 7462

92 A Very English Scandal, John Preston, Penguin 2016 P272

93 Ibid P273

94 From Beyond Discussion, Review by Neal Ascherson in the London Review of Books, 3 April 1980 of The Last Word, An Eye Witness Account of the Thorpe Trial, Aubron Waugh, Joseph 1980

95 Ibid P310

96 Conspiracy of Silence, Freeman and Penrose,Grafton 1986 P367

97 The J C News thejc.com. 7 June 2018

98 In My Own Time, Jeremy Thorpe. Politico's Publishing 1999, P27

99 In My Own Time, Jeremy Thorpe. Politico's Publishing 1999, P31

100 John Anthony Dyson, Lord Dyson, British judge and barrister. Master of the Rolls and Head of Civil Justice from 2010-2012. Born 1943, Leeds.

101 Barry Penrose wrote The Pencourt File (with BBC colleague Roger Courtiour) based on information recounted by Harold Wilson, shortly after he had resigned as British prime minister. Wilson had requested contact with the journalists about conspiracies that he claimed had occurred during his period in government

102 Jeremy Thorpe Michael Bloch, Abacus Book , 2014. Kindle edition Location 8020

103 Liberal History News, Spring 2014. Ronald Porter

104 CBE. Commander of the Most Excellent Order of the British Empire (CBE)

105 Marion Thorpe obituary. Independent 13 March 2014

106 Facebook tribute to Marion by George, one of the Globs band. 8 March 2014

Index

Selective Index of important people, places and events in Marion's life.